Fretboard Knowled...
CONTEMPORARY GUITARIST
THE ULTIMATE GUIDE TO MUSIC FOR BLUES, ROCK AND JAZZ GUITARISTS

VIVIAN CLEMENT

Cover photos: Jeff Oshiro
Cover models (left to right, top to bottom):
Matt Simmons, Link Harnsberger,
Martha Widmann, Marta Csotsits,
Ron Manus

Alfred Music
P.O. Box 10003
Van Nuys, CA 91410-0003
alfred.com

ISBN-10: 0-7390-3157-0
ISBN-13: 978-0-7390-3157-5

Table of Contents

Introduction

The goal of this book is to increase your knowledge of the fretboard. Learning how a musical concept relates to patterns on the fretboard will enable you to more easily incorporate it into your guitar playing. Not knowing where you are at all times on your instrument would be like driving without a map—you would always feel insecure about where you are, and unsure of how to get to your destination. Having good fretboard knowledge will help you learn in an organized and time-efficient manner and confidently take charge of your playing.

To get the most out of this book, you must have a good understanding of the fundamentals of music theory. We will be relating this information to the fretboard. It is best to use this text in conjunction with the other books in this series, or other books like them:

> *Theory for the Contemporary Guitarist*
> *Ear Training for the Contemporary Guitarist*
> *Sight-Reading for the Contemporary Guitarist*

Make sure you are familiar with the concepts listed below. Many of them will be reviewed briefly, but it is best if you have studied them before.

> The musical notes, sharps and flats (including enharmonic equivalents)
>
> Scales (and roots or tonics): pentatonic (major and minor), blues, altered blues, the modes of the major scale, harmonic and melodic minor
>
> Keys (major and minor), keynote (the tonic)
>
> Chords, including the diatonic triads and 7th chords of the major scale and harmonic minor scales, extended chords (9th, 11th, 13th) and altered chords
>
> Chord Progressions

This book can be used on its own but it also correlates with *Theory for the Contemporary Guitarist* by Guy Capuzzo and *Ear Training for the Contemporary Guitarist* by Jody Fisher (also published by the National Guitar Workshop and Alfred). As every new topic begins, you will find a symbol that tells you which page in *Theory for the Contemporary Guitarist* to reference for a more detailed theoretical explanation. For example, if you see this symbol...

> TCG 17
>
> ETCG 20–44

...go to page 17 in *Theory for the Contemporary Guitarist* (TCG) and pages 22–44 of *Ear Training for the Contemporary Guitarist* for a more thorough discussion of the theory and ear training examples.

The concept of this book was developed over several years of teaching. It became evident to me that many of my guitar students were overwhelmed with learning lessons on chords and scales, only to forget them once we moved onto something new. Once I began to teach them about the repetitive patterns that existed on the fretboard, students were able to memorize and understand chords and scales much more efficiently. I experienced first hand how this knowledge creates shortcuts to understanding for my beginning students as well as myself. Also, my advanced students have been able to quickly apply these principles to their pre-existing knowledge, allowing many of them (for the first time) to grasp the methodology of the fretboard.

Repetitive patterns are hidden throughout the design of the fretboard. Because the interval between the 3rd and 2nd string (a major 3rd) is different than those between all the other adjacent strings (perfect 4ths), many of the patterns that would otherwise be obvious are obscured.   This book will help you see them clearly.

By understanding these repetitive patterns, you will be able to increase your ability to manipulate scales and chords. Grouping similar repetitive patterns together allows you to create a systematic way of speeding up memorization.   Memorizing scales and chords is of the utmost importance, and understanding how they relate to patterns and how they affect all of our playing cannot be emphasized enough.

Enjoy discovering the secrets of the fretboard!

About the Author

Vivian Clement is a versitile guitarist whose style ranges from jazz to blues to pop. She studied jazz at Humber College in Toronto with Peter Harris as well as vocals with classical/pop teacher Helen Knight. During the summer months she teaches guitar at the Toronto Campus of the National Guitar workshop as well as privately. Presently she keeps busy performing in the Southern Ontario region and owns and records at Exodus Studio with her husband Anthony Paiano. She has released several CDs.

Thanks

Thanks to Jody Fisher for the encouragement to put my ideas into writing. Also to Brian Murray for all his hard work throughout the year and Nat Gunod for the opportunity to write this book.

Chapter 1—Fretboard Frenzy

Fretboard knowledge is foundational to the advancing guitarist since understanding all scales and chords requires first knowing where to locate and identify the notes. Due to the great amount of notes that are available on the guitar, memorizing them can be quite an undertaking. Sometimes even seasoned players are unable to randomly choose any note and name it, particularly above the 12th fret. In this chapter, you will learn a strategy for dealing with this issue.

TRADITIONAL FRETBOARD METHOD

When deciding to memorize the fretboard, many people simply single out the individual notes and play them, repeating until memorized. This is a random and difficult way to proceed and not recommended.

As a reference for the discussion that follows, this diagram shows all the notes as they appear on the fretboard.

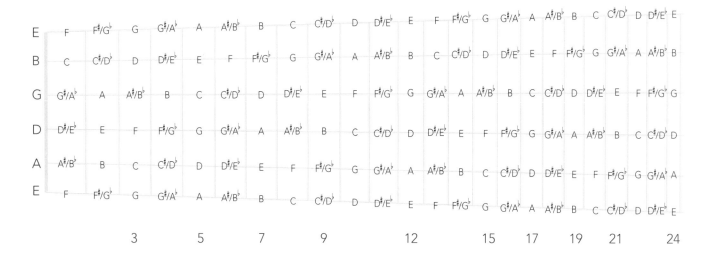

As you can see, the amount of notes to commit to memory is overwhelming, which is why many players only memorize the first few frets or a few favored strings.

If you have spent anytime at all playing the piano, you quickly realized how easy it was to learn the keyboard. It is visually laid out before you; there is a continual repeating pattern of black and white notes that extends from the lowest note to the highest. Although the guitar fretboard does not seem as visually simple, there are definite hidden repetitive patterns that, once revealed, enable the guitarist to see musical constructs throughout its entire length. This allows for easier memorization and a more systematic approach to learning notes, scales and chords.

THE WARPED W

Finding a pattern on the fretboard and learning how it repeats makes memorizing it easier, since we only need to learn it once and then *transpose* it (change its pitch level) as needed.

F NOTES

The following diagram illustrates where all the F notes, in all octaves, are situated throughout the entire fretboard.

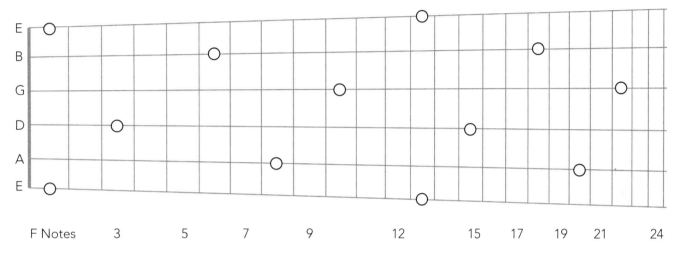

If we draw a line through the notes, joining them all together, a visual pattern emerges from the 1st fret to the 12th fret. It looks like a warped W. The same pattern reoccurs from the 12th fret to the 24th fret, an octave higher.

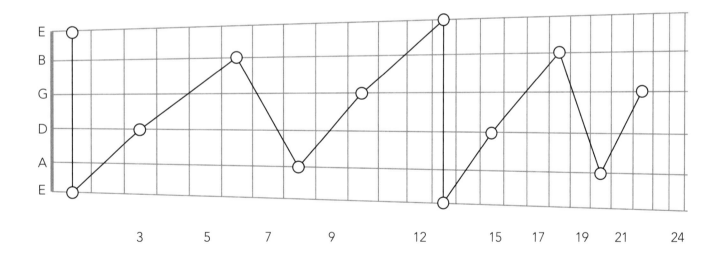

The diagrams in this book have 24 frets in order to demonstrate complete patterns.
The number of frets on guitars varies according to the style of guitar.

We will now create a numerical sequence, assigning each note a number representing its position in relation to all the other F notes in the pattern. There are six notes in the warped W pattern (highlighted in gray), although the sixth does not recur in the higher octave.

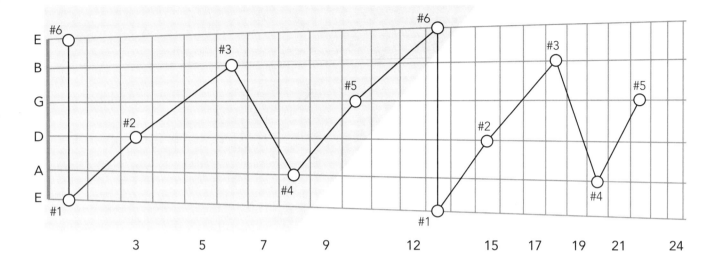

If you randomly choose any F note on this graph, you will be able to find the next F above or below by simply observing which number it is in the sequence and moving up or down in order through the warped W pattern. For example, if you choose the F on the 4th string, 3rd fret— #2 on the sequence—you can find the next F by going down to #1 or up to #3.

The warped W pattern is effective because if we commit it to memory, we need not learn 126 or so individual notes on the fretboard. We can find any note at any time using the pattern. The key is to spend the necessary time to familiarize yourself with the pattern and the overall flow of how each note within it connects to the next.

TRANSPOSING THE WARPED W

Transposing the pattern is simple. First choose an already familiar note. Determine which number it is in the sequence (where it sits on the W). Then move up or down in the pattern to find the next note of the same name. If you are totally unfamiliar with the locations of any notes, you can refer to the diagram in the Traditional Fretboard Method section on page 6.

Here is the warped W pattern for G notes:

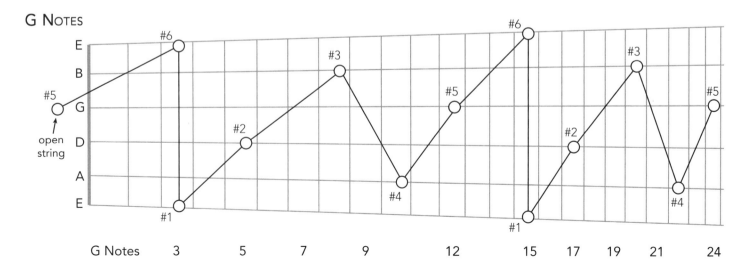

The warped W of G notes (bottom of page 8) starts at the 3rd fret and ends at the 15th fret. It then repeats from the 15th through 24th fret. It doesn't matter where you start on the pattern, the sequence of numbered notes will remain the same.   The only thing that changes when you shift the pattern elsewhere on the fretboard is the names of the notes.

After having practiced this for a while, you will become able to instantly visualize this pattern on the fretboard, making it a breeze to locate any note.   Keep in mind that this is simply a tool for memorization.   If you use this method consistently, it will soon become unnecessary because you will have subconsciously memorized the locations of the notes.

Let's take a look at some other notes. When you have studied these, try doing the same with sharp/flat notes (refer to the diagram in the Traditional Fretboard Method section on page 6 as necessary).

A NOTES

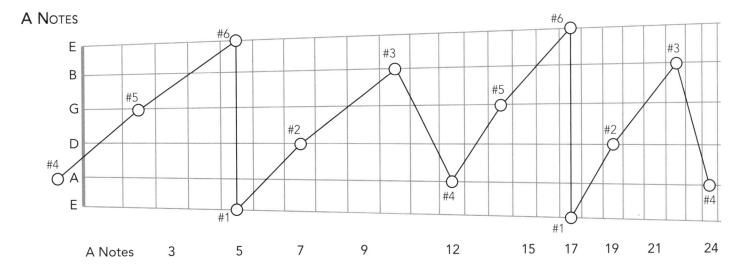

B NOTES

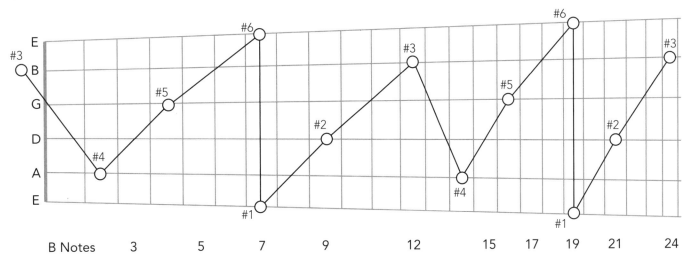

C Notes

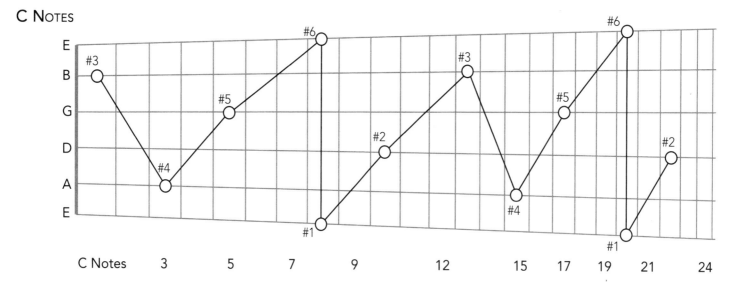

D Notes

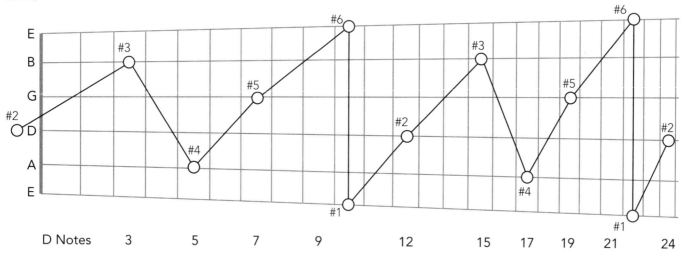

E Notes

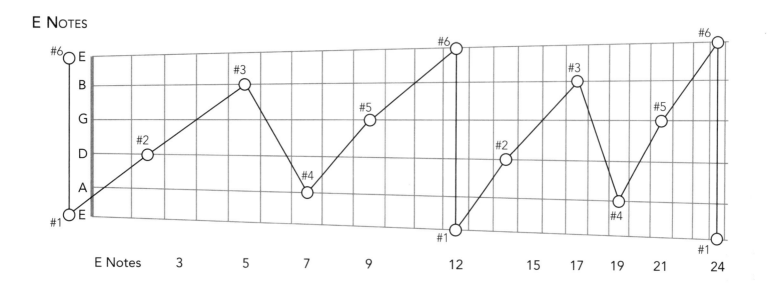

Chapter 2—Pentatonic Scales

TCG 44–45
ETCG 49, 51

Pentatonic scales are the most commonly used scales for soloing in contemporary music. The two most popular pentatonic scales are the major and minor pentatonic scales. We will start with the minor pentatonic scale, which is used primarily to improvise over blues, rock or pop songs with minor chord progressions where the key note is the same as the root (tonic) of the scale. For example, if a song is in C Minor we use a C Minor Pentatonic scale.

Theory Nugget

Any scale can be understood by comparing it to the major scale and observing the differences (or alterations). For example, ♭3 would indicate that the third note in a scale is one half step lower than that of the major scale. If we think of the major scale as being 1(R)–2–3–4–5–6–7–8(1), the minor pentatonic scale, which has only five notes, can be understood as being 1–♭3–4–5–♭7.

TRADITIONAL MINOR PENTATONIC BOX PATTERNS

The conventional method of learning pentatonic scales is to study and memorize the box patterns shown below.

Box Pattern 1

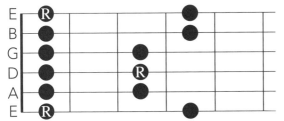

Box Pattern 2

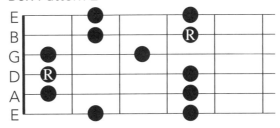

Box Pattern 3

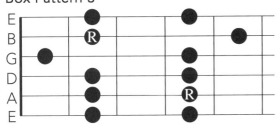

Box Pattern 4

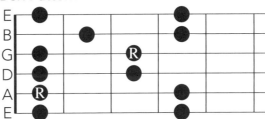

Box Pattern 5

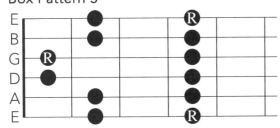

R = Root (tonic)

All patterns are played from left to right starting on the lowest string (in the case of these box patterns, the 6th string). These patterns can be played in any key by simply starting on the desired root. It is very important, therefore, to know the locations of the roots in the patterns and the names of the notes on the fretboard.

These are the most commonly used minor pentatonic scale patterns and they can take a considerable amount of time to memorize, since there are no memorable visible repeating patterns.

FOUR-NOTE REPETITIVE MINOR PENTATONIC CELLS

Since repetitive patterns for notes appear throughout the fretboard, we can deduct that patterns also appear in regard to scales as well. The following illustrations are cells from which we will build our minor pentatonic scales. The notes in the cellss are connected by lines. It is important to become familiar with the relationship of the root to the other notes in the various cells, therefore making it easy to transpose to any root anywhere on the fretboard.

Cell 1 starts on the root and goes to the right.

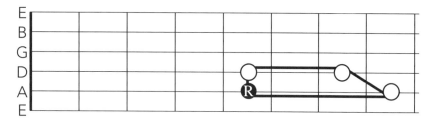

The root for **Cell 2** is not in the circle but will be used as a *joining note* (later, joining notes will help us connect these patterns). Joining notes are square. This pattern is above and to the left of the root.

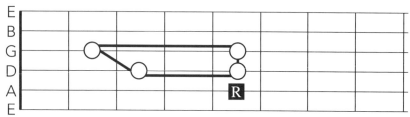

Cell 3 starts to the left and below the root, which is the fourth note.

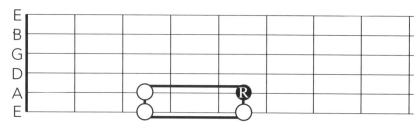

Cell 4 is below the root and has the root as its third note.

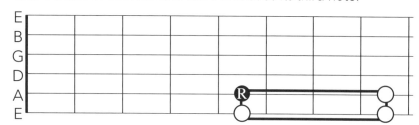

Cell 5 is above the root and has the root as its second note.

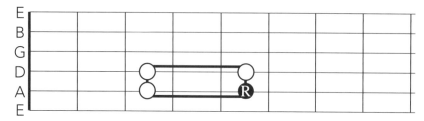

This key will help you interpret the diagrams on the following pages.

 = Traditional box pattern note
Ⓡ = Root
○ = Repetitive cell note
■ = Joining note

You can view these cells together on the fretboard in different ways. Here, all five of these cells are created around only one root.

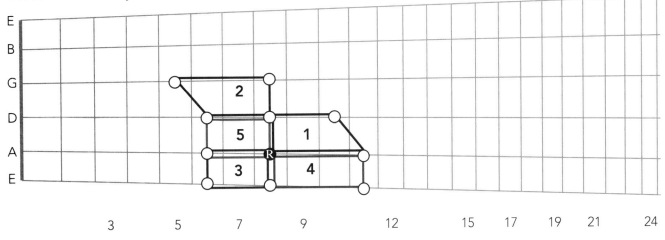

The five cells can be found most anywhere a root is located.

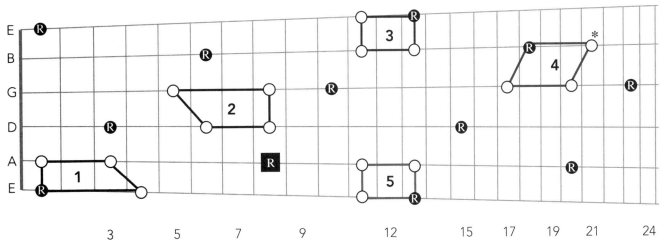

* Since the 3rd and 2nd strings are tuned a major 3rd apart rather than a perfect 4th like all the other strings, you will have to compensate by raising the notes of the 2nd string up one fret (more on this later).

Now connect Cell 1 to create a repetitive minor pentatonic scale pattern.

USING REPETITIVE CELL 1

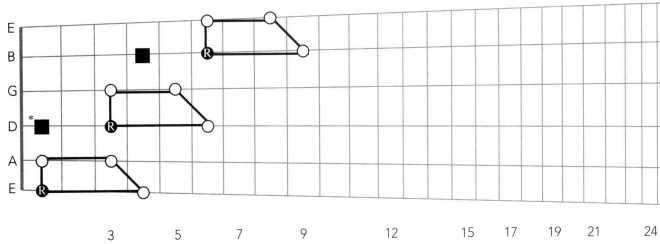

This scale pattern is made up of three repetitions of Cell 1 on page 12. Compared to the box patterns, this is a lot quicker to memorize and covers the same notes.

* The square notes are joining notes that connect all the cells together.

REPETITIVE MINOR PENTATONIC SCALE FORM—VERSION ONE

Now we will observe how these repetitive cells relate to the traditional box patterns.

In this diagram, Cell 1 is related to Box Patterns numbers 1, 2 and 3.

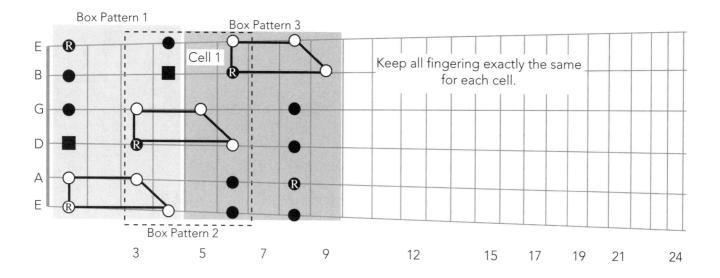

Notice how Cell 1 crosses through Box Patterns numbers 1, 2 and 3. This compounds your soloing possibilities. You can choose to solo using this new, repetitive pattern or jump in and out of any of the box patterns. This takes a little bit of practice, but once you are familiar with these patterns you will discover that you are not limited to sticking to only one. Many guitarists who have studied the Box Patterns complain of always having to "play in the box." This simply means they feel trapped in one pattern and are unable to come up with new and fresh ideas for soloing. The repetitive patterns help eliminate this problem by offering you more options from which to choose.

This diagram shows how Repetitive Cell 2 crosses through Box Patterns numbers 2, 3 and 4. Cell 2 is the trickiest one to use since the root is actually the joining note and not in the pattern itself.

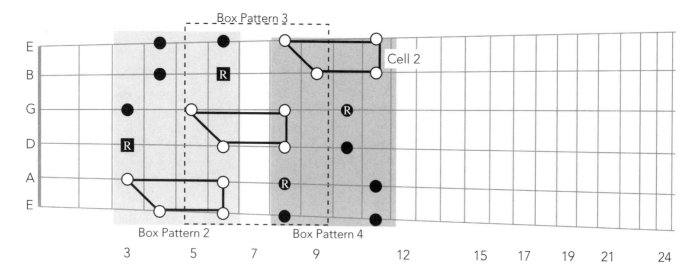

This diagram shows how Cell 3 crosses through Box Patterns numbers 3, 4 and 5.

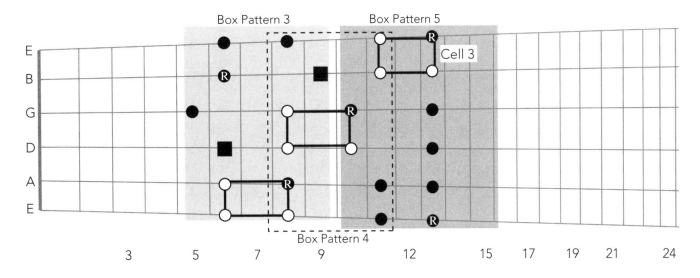

The next diagram shows how Cell 4 crosses through Box Patterns numbers 4, 5 and 1 (#1 is up an octave).

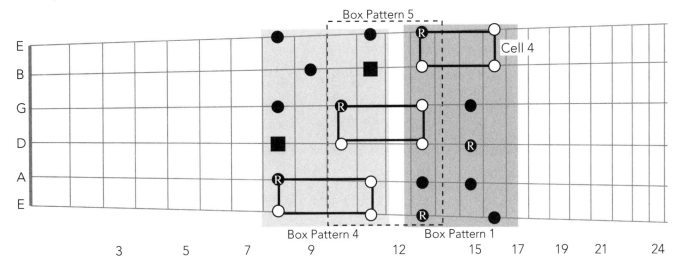

Notice that the scale forms we are creating for the minor pentatonic scale, using the different Repetitive Minor Pentatonic Scale patterns, all overlap. You are learning a system that integrates the entire fretboard.

This diagram shows how Cell 5 crosses through Box Patterns numbers 5, 1 and 2. Cell 5 is similar to Cell 3 except for the joining note which is one fret over to the left.

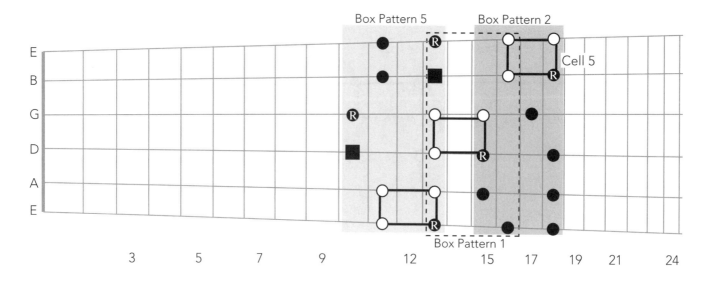

If you are already familiar with the box patterns for the minor pentatonic scale, you will be able to incorporate these alternate scale patterns into your playing. They don't replace traditional box patterns but increase your options for improvising and present a different approach to understanding repetitive patterns.

CONCLUSIONS AND REVIEW:

1. You can create any pattern whatsoever using two strings and then duplicate it throughout the fretboard by adding a joining note to connect them. The only adjustment you will have to make is to raise the 2nd string notes one half step (one fret to the right).

2. You are not limited to playing the whole pattern from start to finish. You can start playing anywhere in a box and using a pattern of two strings move into the next box pattern or play a cell.

3. Each of the five repetitive cells are identical to the beginning five notes of each of the traditional box patterns. For example, Cell 1 is same as the first five notes of Box Pattern 1.

4. Each cell runs through three of the box patterns, allowing you to move in and out of any box pattern as you solo. This gives you many more options from which to chose and makes it easier to play up and down the entire fretboard.

REPETITIVE MINOR PENTATONIC SCALE FORM—VERSION TWO

Version Two of the Repetitive Minor Pentatonic Scale Form is a little trickier but offers further choices for soloing. It uses the exact same five patterns as Version One, but they appear on different string groupings. The notes played on the 2nd string will need to be moved up one fret to compensate for the tuning. While this slightly alters the pattern, it is conceptually the same.

This diagram illustrates how Cell 1 crosses through Box Pattern numbers 3, 4 and 5. (In Version One it crosses through Box Pattern numbers 1, 2 and 3.)

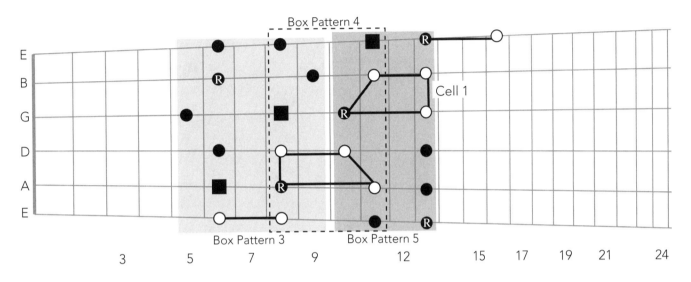

It is vitally important that you are able to see that these patterns are the same as in Version One of the Repetitive Minor Pentatonic scale, but are altered only because of the tuning of the 2nd string.

Also take notice that the 6th string and 1st strings have portions of Cell 1.

Although Version Two is more difficult to grasp initially, it is an important scale form to learn. By memorizing only Version One and Two of these Repetitive Minor Pentatonic scale forms, you can cross through all five of the box patterns. This allows you access to any box pattern at any time while soloing, thus further solving the problem of getting "stuck in a box."

In Version Two, Cell 2 runs through Box Pattern numbers 4, 5 and 1.   Again, the 1st and 6th strings have partial patterns. The root of this pattern is also the joining note.

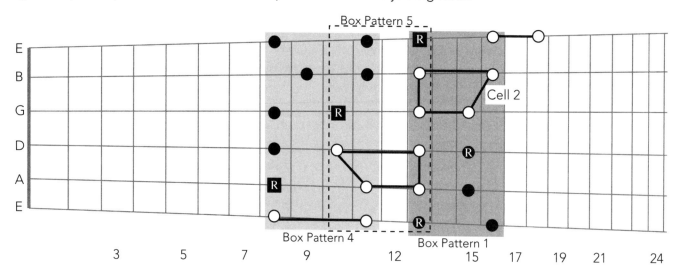

Cell 3 runs through numbers 5, 1 and 2 of the box patterns. Remember to also memorize the partial patterns appearing on the 6th and 1st strings.

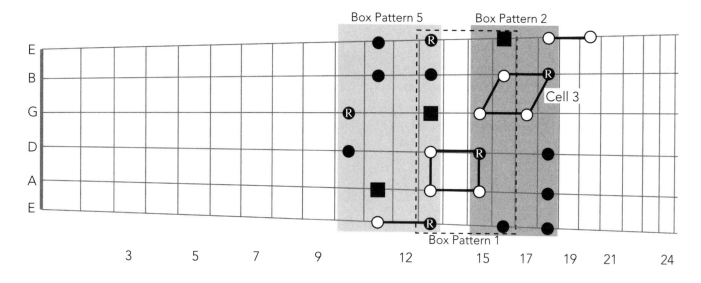

Once you have reached the end of the fretboard on any of these scale forms, as we did in the last diagram, you will need to start over again at the beginning of the fretboard. Cell 4 crosses Box Pattern numbers 1, 2 and 3, and has partial patterns on the 1st and 6th string.

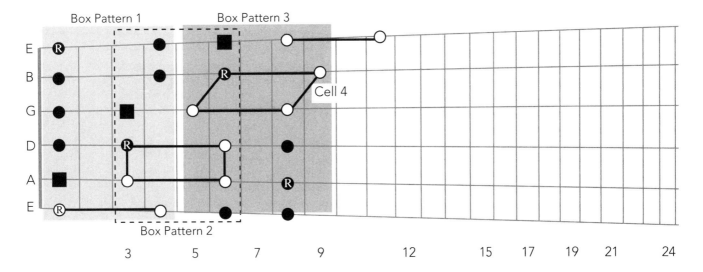

Cell 5 runs through Box Pattern numbers 2, 3 and 4 with partial patterns on the 1st and 6th strings. It's important to always remember where the roots are located in the repetitive patterns. This enables you to play any pattern you wish and never lose your place.

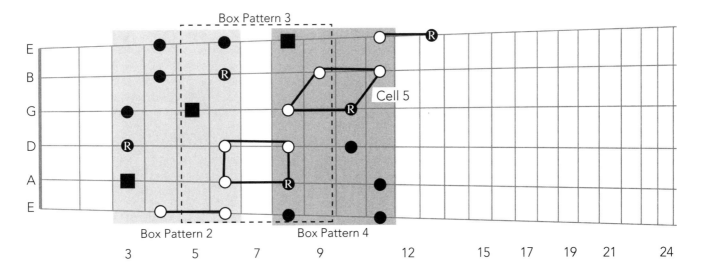

PUTTING IT ALL TOGETHER—VERSIONS ONE AND TWO

Let's take a look at what Versions One and Two of the Repetitive Minor Pentatonic Scale forms look like side by side. As you will see, the two scale forms cover a wide range and allow you access to the entire fretboard, helping to keep you from being stuck in only one area. As you begin to practice the repetitive cells and scale forms you will become more confident in your ability to solo throughout the entire fretboard and move in and out of any traditional box pattern. For the sake of consistency, Version One (in light gray rectangles) will always be followed by Version Two (in darker gray rectangles) in the following diagrams.

COMBINED SCALE FORM 1

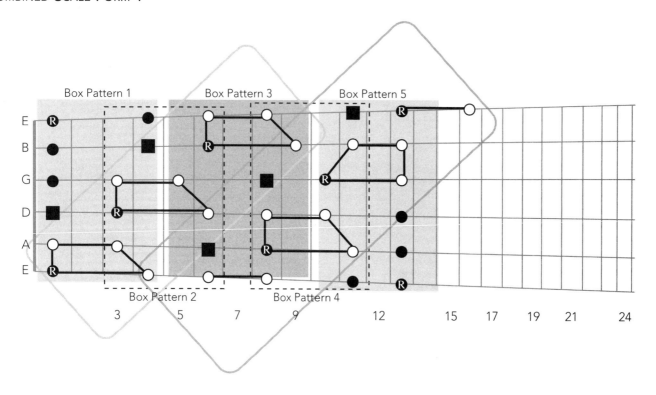

COMBINED SCALE FORM 2

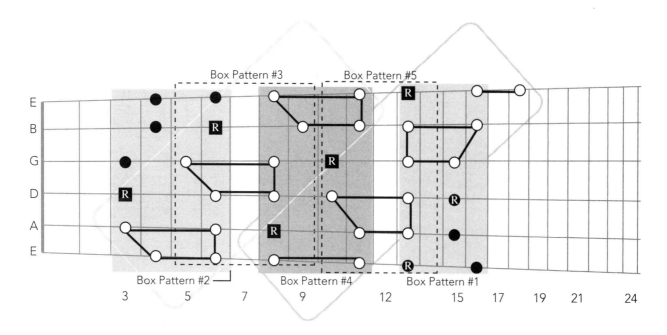

COMBINED SCALE FORM 3

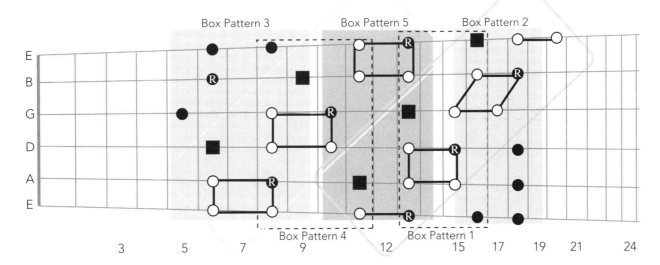

COMBINED SCALE FORM 4

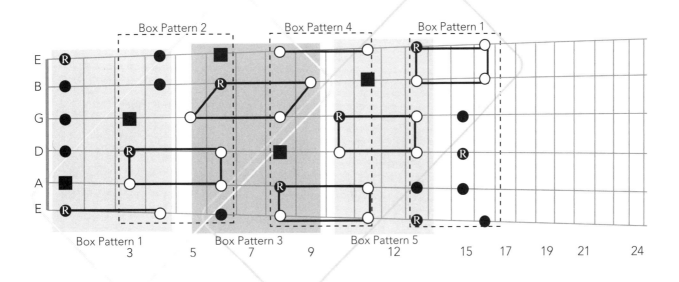

COMBINED SCALE FORM 5

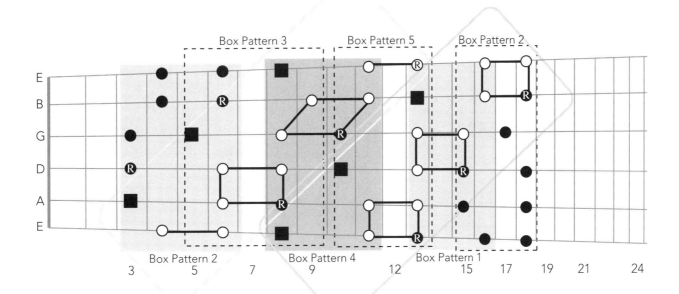

THE BLUES SCALE—VERSIONS ONE AND TWO

TCG 47–49
ETCG 50–51

Before we leave the minor pentatonic scale, we don't want to forget a very important variation: the blues scale. As the name suggests, the blues scale is a popluar tool for soloing in a blues context but it can also be used in rock and pop. As with any scale, you can experiment with it in many styles of music to see how it might work.

Since you are already familiar with the way the previous repetitive scale forms were built, we will simply illustrate the blues scale in Versions One and Two of the full repetitive scale forms. To create box patterns for the blues scale, simply add a ♭5 (one half step above the fourth note or below the fifth note) to each of the minor pentatonic box patterns on page 11. Blues Scale Forms Versions One and Two will be crossing through all the traditional blues box patterns.

The altered blues scale, which adds a ♮7 to the blues scale, will also add an edge to your improvising. You could substitute the altered blues scale for the blues scale when soloing over a blues progression (see the above Theory Nugget on this page for formula for an altered blues scale). The diagrams on this page and the next are for the regular, unaltered blues scale.

Theory Nugget

The blues scale is exactly like the minor pentatonic Scale except that is has an added ♭5. The formula is: 1–♭3–4–♭5–5–♭7. The formula for the altered blues scale is: 1–♭3–♭5–5–♭7–♮7.

COMBINED BLUES SCALE FORM 1

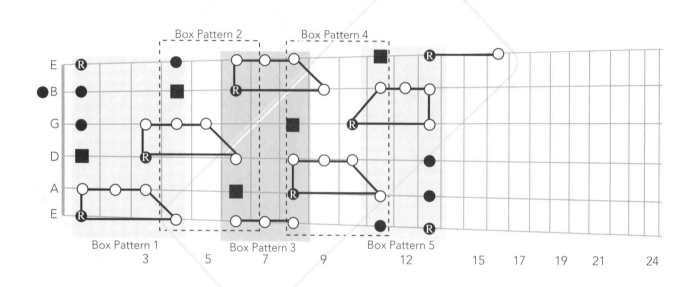

COMBINED BLUES SCALE FORM 2

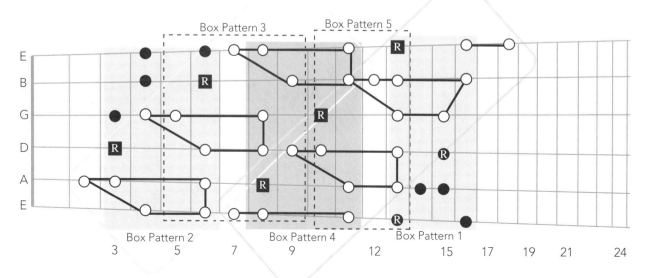

COMBINED BLUES SCALE FORM 3

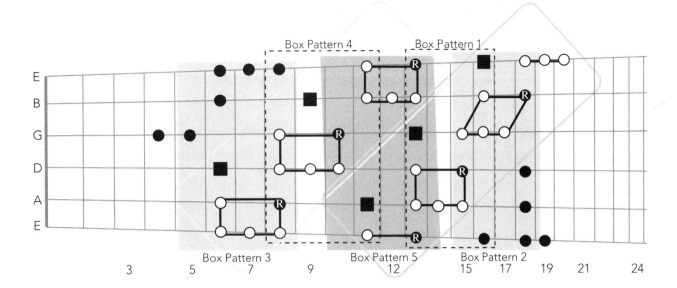

COMBINED BLUES SCALE FORM 4

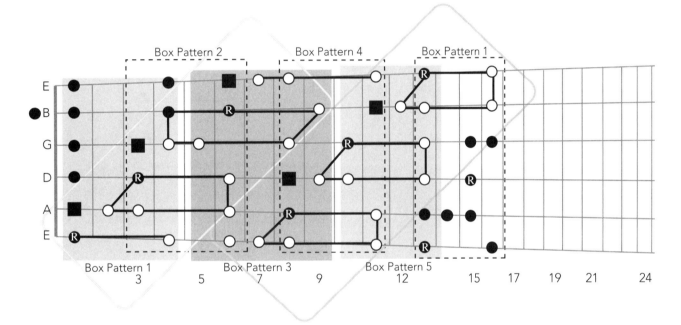

COMBINED BLUES SCALE FORM 5

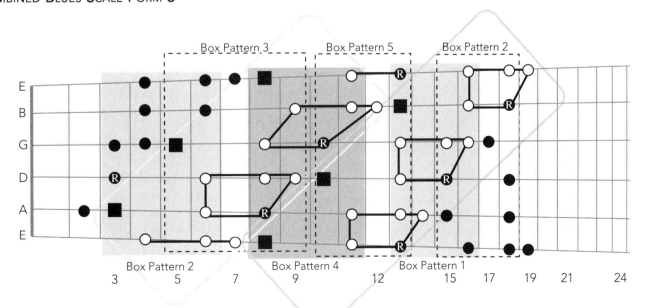

Chapter 3—Pentatonic Plus

TCG 44–46
ETCG 49

Now that you have a good grasp of the minor pentatonic scale on the fretboard, let's look at the major pentatonic scale. The major pentatonic scale is also quite popular and is used for soloing over major-sounding blues, pop, rock and country. It works well over dominant, major and major 7th chords.

Note that the major and minor pentatonic scale box patterns are exactly the same except for the locations of the roots. There is also a very distinct difference in the sound of these scales when they are played in context.

Theory Nugget

The major pentatonic scale is created by also using only five notes of the major scale: 1–2–3–5–6. It also has a relative relationship to the minor pentatonic scale. In other words, the C Major Pentatonic scale has exactly the same notes as the A Minor Pentatonic scale; only the roots are different.

TRADITIONAL MAJOR PENTATONIC BOX PATTERNS

Box Pattern 1

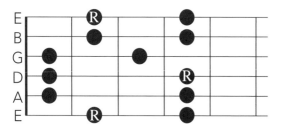

Major Pentatonic Box Pattern 1 is the same as Minor Pentatonic Box Pattern #2.

Box Pattern 2

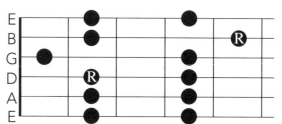

This pattern is exactly the same as Minor Pentatonic Box Pattern 3.

Box Pattern 3

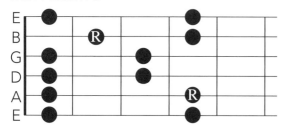

Major Pentatonic Box Pattern 3 is exactly the same as Minor Pentatonic Box Pattern 4.

Box Pattern 4

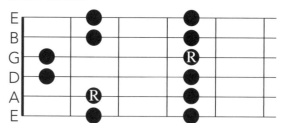

Major Pentatonic Box Pattern 4 is the same as Minor Pentatonic Box Pattern 5.

Box Pattern 5

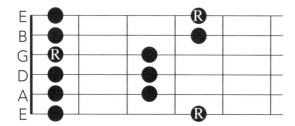

This pattern is the same as Minor Pentatonic Box Pattern 1.

As with the minor pentatonic patterns, these can be played in any key by moving the roots to the desired notes. You need only know the locations of the roots in the patterns and the names of the notes on the fretboard.

FOUR-NOTE REPETITIVE MAJOR PENTATONIC PATTERNS

Let's now examine the five repetitive major pentatonic patterns.

Major Pentatonic Cell 1 starts on the root and goes to the right.

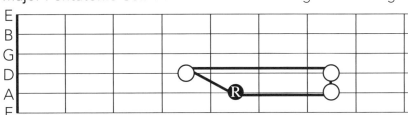

The root of **Major Pentatonic Cell 2** is not in the connected pattern but is situated over to the left.

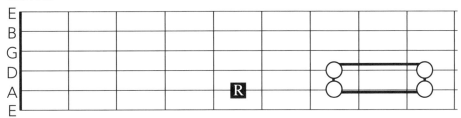

Major Pentatonic Cell 3 starts to the left and below the root and ends on the root.

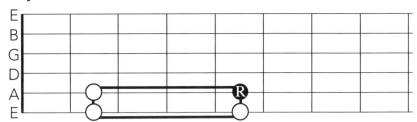

Major Pentatonic Cell 4 is below the root and has the root as its third note.

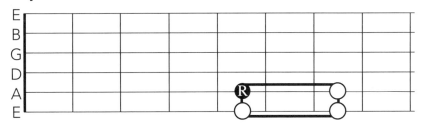

Major Pentatonic Cell 5 is above the root and has the root as its second note.

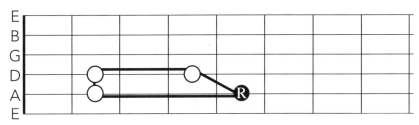

REPETITIVE MAJOR PENTATONIC SCALE FORM— VERSIONS ONE AND TWO

The following major pentatonic scales combine the Repetitive Patterns Version One and Two. Version One appears as the first pattern to the left in the diagram. The box patterns referenced in the diagrams are those on page 24.

COMBINED MAJOR PENTATONIC SCALE FORM 1

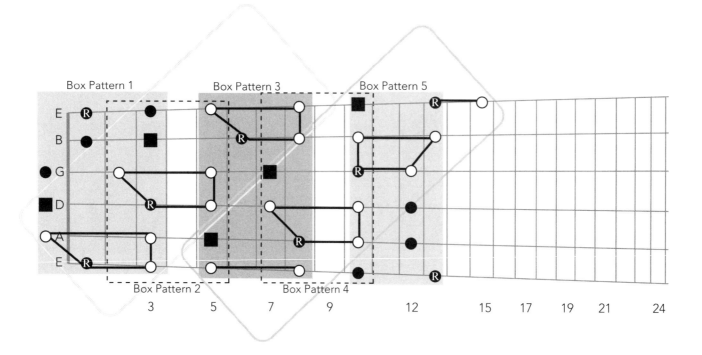

COMBINED MAJOR PENTATONIC SCALE FORM 2

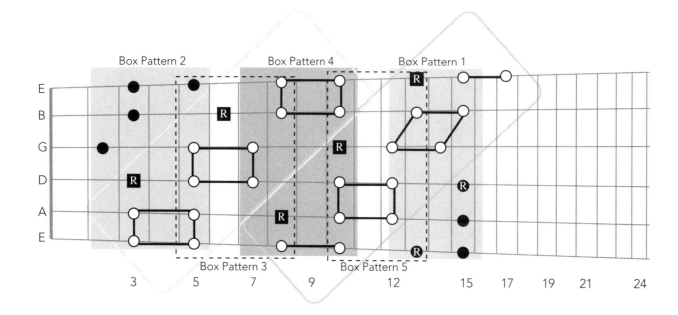

COMBINED MAJOR PENTATONIC SCALE FORM 3

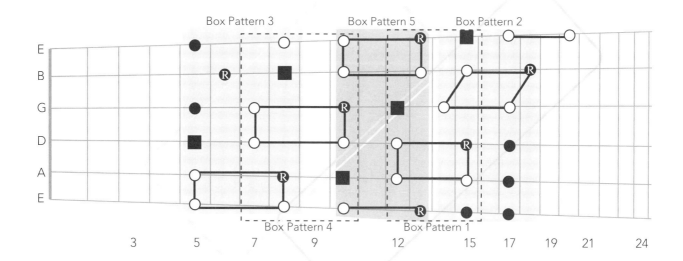

COMBINED MAJOR PENTATONIC SCALE FORM 4

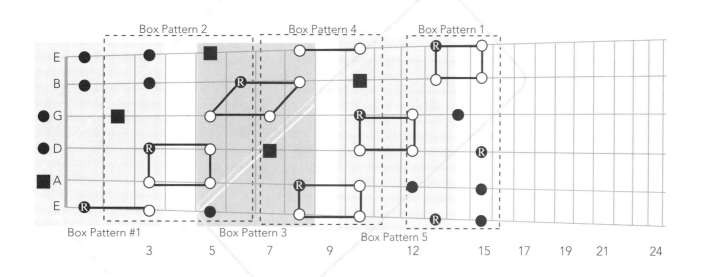

COMBINED MAJOR PENTATONIC SCALE FORM 5

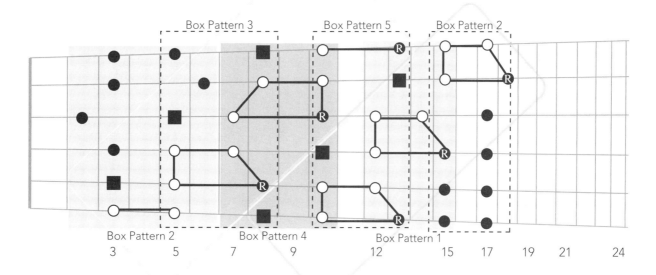

Chapter 4–Modes and Minor Scales

TCG 53–57
ETCG 62–67

The modes of the major scale can be traced as far back as ancient Greece, and the names are believed to have been derived from the place-names that ancient Greek theorists associated with them. Refer to pages 53–57 in *Theory for the Contemporary Guitarist* by Guy Capuzzo for a thorough discussion of these modes. In this chapter we will be presenting them from the perspective of repetitive patterns on the fretboard.

Simply put, modes are used to create moods in songs. The major sounding modes create an "up," happy mood because they have a major 3rd. These are the Ionian, Lydian and Mixolydian modes. The darker, more melancholy modes have a minor 3rd. They are the Dorian, Phrygian, Aeolian and Locrian modes.

In order to get a good grasp on modes, you'll need to spend time playing and listening to them in various musical contexts and experiment with which modes work with which chord progressions. For example, the Ionian and Lydian modes are commonly used in rock when a major sounding mode is needed. For a darker sound in rock, you may use the Dorian or Aeolian mode. In jazz, there are many modes and scales that can be used depending on the mood and movement of the progression. For a complete discussion of jazz improvisation with the modes, and many other devices, check out *The Big Book of Jazz Guitar Improvisation*, by Mark Dziuba or *The Complete Jazz Guitar Method* by Jody Fisher.

There are generally two approaches to viewing modes: parallel or derivative. In the parallel approach, the modes are viewed as a modification of the major scale while in the derivative approach, each mode is a different reordering of the major scale.

Theory Nugget

Each mode has its own unique sound, which is determined by where the half steps fall in the scale. The half steps for the modes of the major scale are as follows:

Ionian	3–4 and 7–1
Dorian	2–3 and 6–7
Phrygian	1–2 and 5–6
Lydian	4–5 and 7–1
Mixolydian	3–4 and 6–7
Aeolian	2–3 and 5–6
Locrian	1–2 and 4–5

Keep in mind that the Ionian mode is exactly the same as the major scale, which is the most important scale for you to know, because all others are derived from or compared to it.

THE DERIVATIVE APPROACH

TCG 53

ETCG 63

IONIAN

In the derivative approach to creating or viewing the modes, each mode is a different rearrangement of a major scale. For example, the Ionian mode is the major scale starting and ending on the first note of a major scale. If it is a C Major scale, we would start on C and end on C an octave higher. This is the C Ionian mode and, obviously, it is exactly the same as the C Major scale.

The Ionian mode is relatively bright and happy sounding. It is commonly used for pop, country and some ethnic music (South American or Latin, Italian and French, for example) and is played over major, major 7th or power chords with the same root.

> **Theory Nugget**
> The Ionian mode has half steps between 3–4 (E–F) and 7–1 (B–C).

Here is an example of a C Ionian Mode on the fretboard of the guitar. Keep in mind that there are various ways of playing modes, which we will discuss at length later in the chapter. The slurs show the locations of the half steps in the scale form.

⌣ = Half step.

◯ = This note is on the next lower or higher adjacent string in the pattern. It's shown here to help clarify the location of a half step.

C Ionian

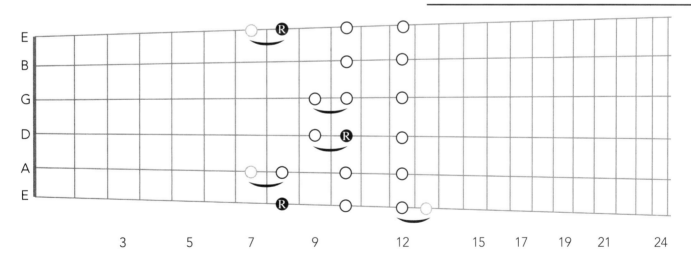

The G Ionian mode works well with the example chord progression below. To transpose the scale form shown above to G, just move it down to begin on the 3rd fret of the 6th string. Try recording the example chord progressions given in this book and practice soloing over them.

TCG 53
ETCG 63

DORIAN

The second mode we will examine is the Dorian mode, which has a minor 3rd and minor 7th above its root. This mode is brighter-sounding than the other minor modes. It sounds great for blues, rock and jazz and works well over minor 7th chords or power chords with the same root.

Theory Nugget

The Dorian mode has half steps between 2–3 (E–F) and 6–7 (B–C). Notice how the names of the notes in D Dorian are the same as in C Ionian, only their positions in the mode are different.

When derived from the C Major scale, the Dorian mode starts on the D, the second note of the scale, and ends on the D one octave higher. Here it is on the fretboard, with slurs marking the half steps.

D Dorian

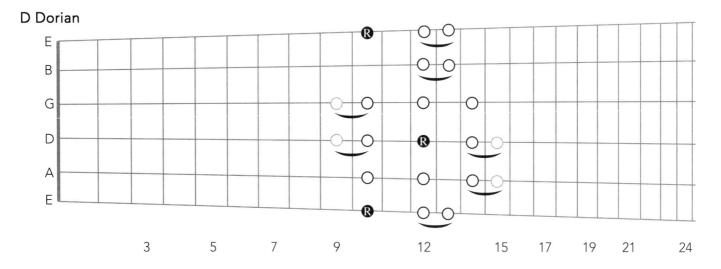

Practice improvising with an A Dorian Mode over this bluesy jazz progression. Move the scale form above down to the 5th fret to transpose it to A.

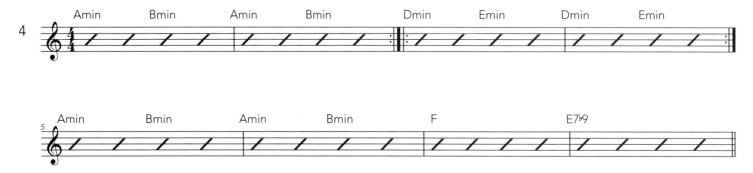

PHRYGIAN

Phrygian, which begins on the third note of the major scale, is a fairly dark-sounding minor mode and has quite a haunting sound created by the half step between the first and second notes. You will need to test the waters with this one to see where it fits in best. It is mostly used over jazz progressions, in progressive rock and in dark-sounding heavy metal tunes.

TCG 54

ETCG 64

Theory Nugget

The Phrygian mode has half steps between 1–2 (E–F) and 5–6 (B–C)

Here is the E Phrygian mode of the C Major scale on the fretboard with slurs marking the half steps.

E Phrygian

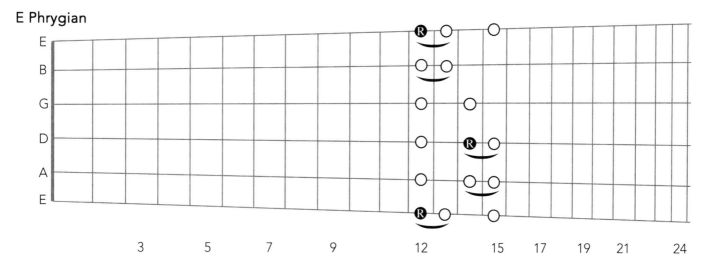

Here is a chord progression over which you can practice soloing with C Phrygian. To transpose the E Phrygian scale form shown above to C, simply move it down to the 8th fret.

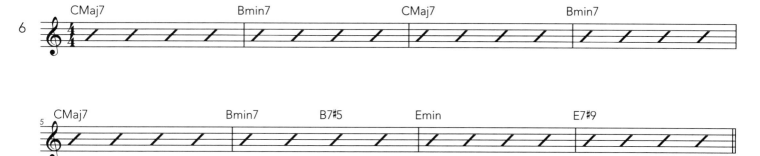

Lydian

Lydian is the brightest-sounding major mode of the major scale. It begins on the fourth note of the major scale. While it takes some time to get used to the whole step between its third and fourth notes, it works well over major and major 7th chords. It is primarily used in jazz and some progressive rock.

TCG 59

ETCG 65

Theory Nugget

The Lydian mode's half steps are between 4–5 (B–C) and 7–1 (E–F).

F Lydian

7

Below is the F Lydian mode of the C Major scale on the fretboard with slurs marking the half steps. Since we are getting higher up on the fretboard, this mode was transposed an octave lower for easier playability. Notice that in this position, two of the notes are played on the open 1st and 2nd string.

F Lydian

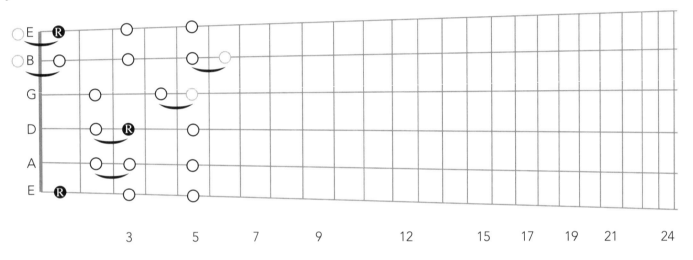

You can play F Lydian over the rock progression shown below.

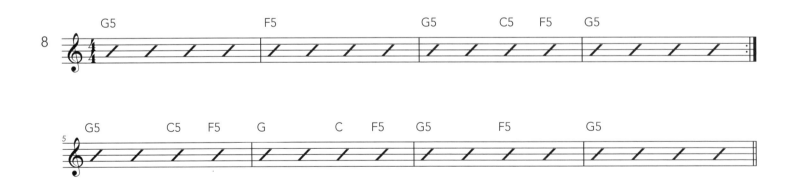

MIXOLYDIAN

TCG 54

ETCG 66

The Mixolydian mode, which is built on the fifth note of the major scale, is the least bright-sounding of the major modes. This is because it has a minor 7th above the root, which makes it sound more dominant than major. You can use Mixolydian to solo over basic rock 'n' roll and blues. It works well over dominant 7th chords, major triads and power chords with the same root.

Theory Nugget
The Mixolydian mode's half steps are between 3–4 (B–C) and 6–7 (E–F).

G Mixolydian

Here is the G Mixolydian mode of the C Major scale with slurs marking the half steps.

G Mixolydian

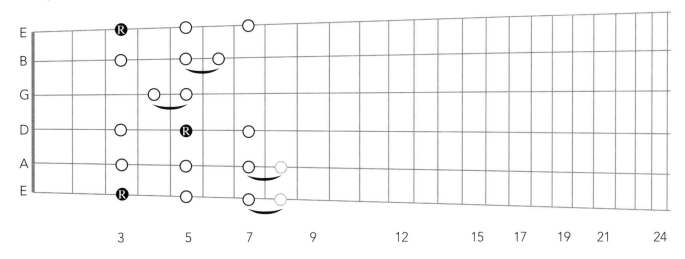

You can use a C Mixolydian to solo over this blues/funk progression. Simply transpose the scale form shown above up to the 8th fret.

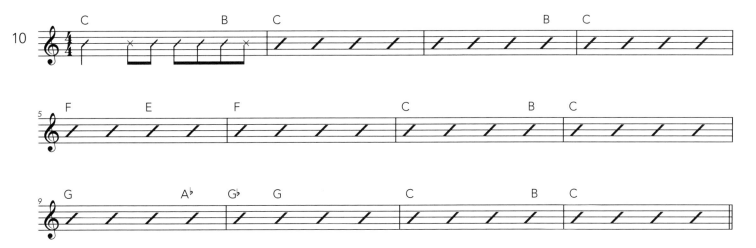

AEOLIAN

TCG 55
ETCG 67

The Aeolian mode is built on the sixth note of the major scale, and is a minor mode. In fact, it is also known as the natural minor scale, the relative minor scale of the major scale. See pages 22 and 23 of *Theory for the Contemporary Guitarist* by Guy Capuzzo for a discussion of this scale and relative minor keys.

Being the most common minor scale, it is widely used in many music styles including pop, various ethnic styles, rock and classical. It is used often over minor triads, minor 7th chords or power chords with the same root.

> **Theory Nugget**
>
> The Aeolian mode has half steps between 2–3 (B–C) and 5–6 (E–F).

Here is the A Aeolian mode of the C Major scale on the fretboard with slurs marking the half steps.

A Aeolian

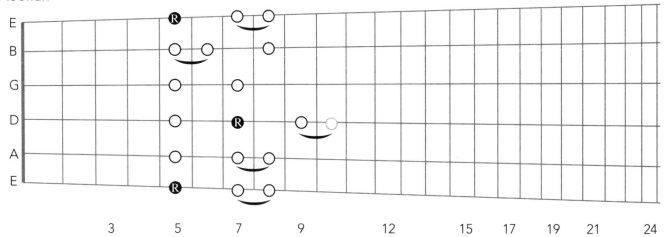

Practice using the C Aeolian mode to improvise over this chord progression. Transpose the scale form shown above to C by moving it up to the 8th fret.

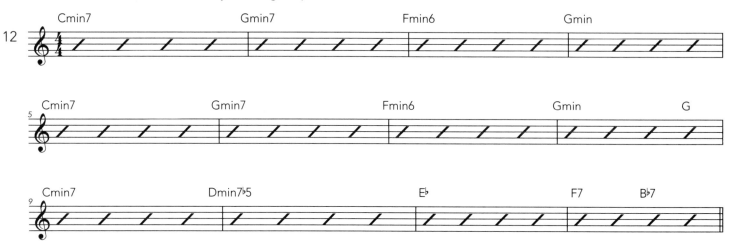

LOCRIAN

The Locrian mode, built on the seventh note of the major scale, is the darkest sounding mode and is very closely related in sound to the Phrygian mode. Locrian can be created by lowering the 5th of the Phrygian mode. Used almost exlusively for jazz and very dark heavy metal, the Locrian mode lends itself well to use over diminished triads and the minor 7♭5 chord with the same root as the mode.

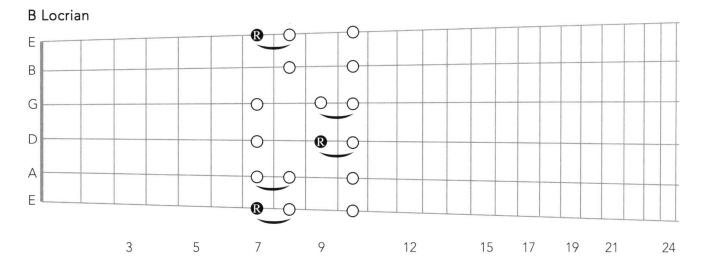

> **TCG 55**
> **ETCG 67**

> ### Theory Nuggets
> The Locrian mode's half steps are between 1–2 (B–C) and 4–5 (E–F).

Here is the B Locrian mode of the C Major scale on the fretboard with slurs marking the half steps.

B Locrian

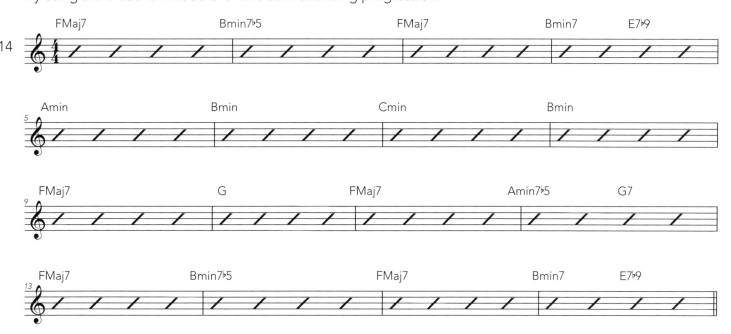

Try using the B Locrian mode over this dark-sounding progression.

THE PARALLEL APPROACH

TCG 53–57
ETCG 62–67

The derivative and parallel approaches are two different ways to few the same modes. In the parallel approach, we observe how a parallel major scale is altered to create the mode. In other words, we use the same root, but change the major scale to make the mode. For example, the G Mixolydian mode is simply a G Major scale with a flatted 7th (♭7). In the derivative approach, we would view the G Mixolydian mode as a C Major scale beginning on G, the 5th degree (page 33).

We represent scale degrees of the major scale with the following numbers 1–2–3–4–5–6–7. The formula for each mode shows the alterations to these notes. For example, the formula for Mixolydian is 1–2–3–4–5–6–♭7.

When putting the modes on the fretboard of the guitar, we can think of a major scale fingering (which is exactly the same as the Ionian mode) and alter it to create modal fingerings. Following, we will look at an F Major (Ionian) scale fingering and alter it to create the other modes of the major scale. The altered notes will be gray. A quick glance will show whether there are lots of alterations or just one or two.

F IONIAN
Formula: 1–2–3–4–5–6–7

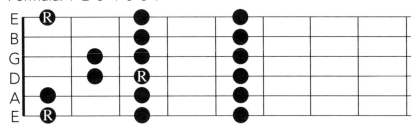

F DORIAN
Formula: 1–2–♭3–4–5–6–♭7

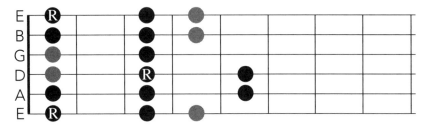

F PHRYGIAN
Formula: 1–♭2–♭3–4–5–♭6–♭7

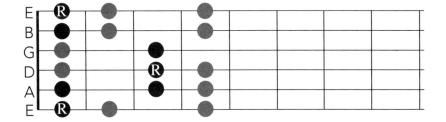

F LYDIAN
Formula: 1–2–3–#4–5–6–7

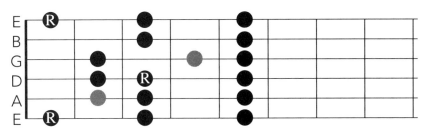

F MIXOLYDIAN
Formula: 1–2–3–4–5–6–♭7

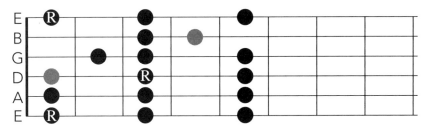

F AEOLIAN
Formula: 1–2–♭3–4–5–♭6–♭7

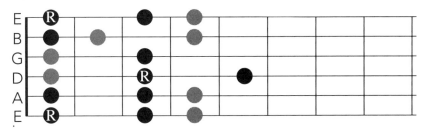

F LOCRIAN
Formula: 1–♭2–♭3–4–♭5–♭6–♭7

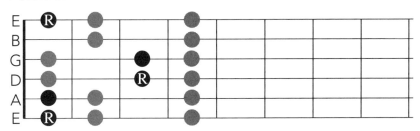

REPETITIVE MODE CELLS

Using a repetitive cell approach will enable you to visually identify the altered notes for each of the modes more easily.

IONIAN

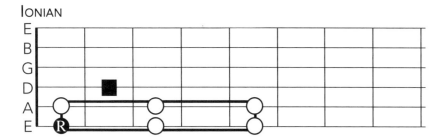

The formula for the Ionian mode, 1–2–3–4–5–6–7, has no altered notes.

DORIAN

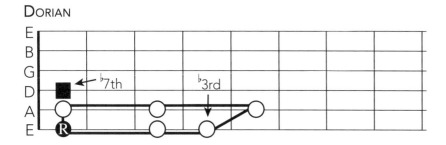

The formula for a Dorian mode is 1–2–♭3–4–5–6–♭7. Comparing this repetitive cell to that of the Ionian makes it easy to see that the 3rd and 7th are altered.

PHRYGIAN

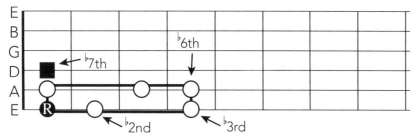

Once again, you can simply compare this repetitive cell to the Ionian's and see what the formula is by observing its flattened notes. The formula is 1–♭2–♭3–4–5–♭6–♭7. Notice that the ♭7 is the joining note.

LYDIAN

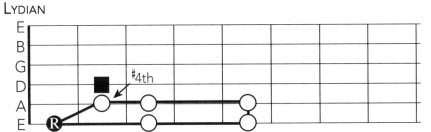

Once again, the Lydian formula (1–2–3–#4–5–6–7) is made very clear by comparing its repetitive cell to that of the Ionian mode. The joining note is 7.

MIXOLYDIAN

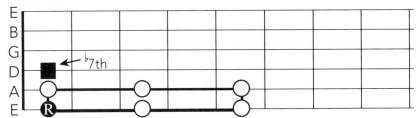

The Mixolydian mode is similar to Lydian in that it has only one altered note, this time being the ♭7. It is identical in every other way to the Ionian: 1–2–3–4–5–6–♭7. The ♭7 is the joining note.

AEOLIAN

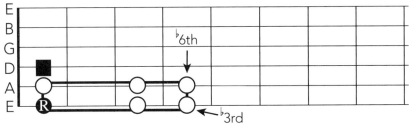

Notice the similarities between the Aeolian and Dorian modes. Aeolian's formula is: 1–2–♭3–4–5–♭6–♭7. Again, the joining note is the ♭7.

LOCRIAN

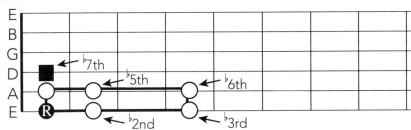

Compared to the Ionian mode, Locrian has every note altered except for 1 and 4: 1–♭2–♭3–4–♭5–♭6–♭7. Once again, the joining note is the ♭7.

MODE PATTERN SIMILARITIES

The power of repetitive patterns and cells on the fretboard becomes obvious when we understand how their visual simplicity makes memorization easier. Let's take a look at the similarities and differences between the following groups of modes. In Group 1, we see that Mixolydian is identical to the Ionian except for the joining note, ♭7, which is lowered one fret. Lydian is identical to the Ionian except for the fourth note, which is raised one fret.

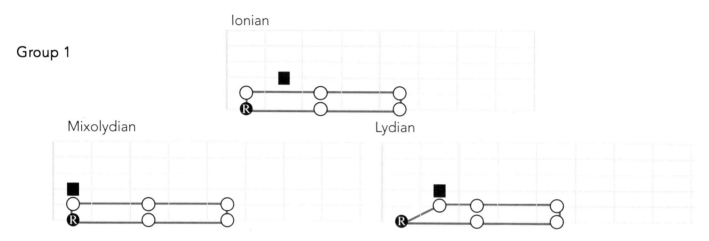

Group 1

In Group 2, we can see that the Dorian is identical to the Aeolian except that the sixth note is raised one fret. Phrygian is identical to the Aeolian except that the second note is lowered one fret.

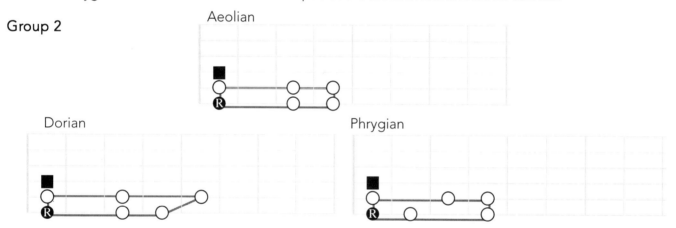

Group 2

In Group 3, notice that Locrian is identical to the Phrygian, except for the fifth note, which is lowered one fret.

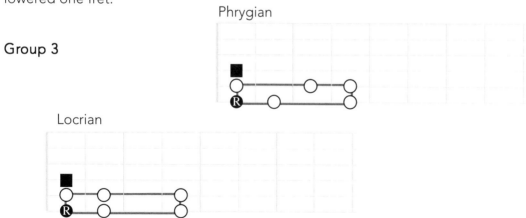

Group 3

Grouping these cells together for memorization enables one to quickly absorb and master modes. The side benefit of this approach is that your ear will naturally begin to hear and identify the subtle differences between the modes. It is always the musician who has the greatest ability to use his or her ear effectively who rises to new levels of understanding and performance with the greatest ease.

REPETITIVE MODE SCALE FORMS—VERSIONS ONE AND TWO

If you have spent time in the past memorizing modes, you are well aware of what a monumental task it can be. Using repetitive patterns will enable you to memorize them very quickly.

We will now join together the repetitive patterns discussed on pages 38–40 to create scale forms. If you have already learned various patterns for modes, you will find that these cover the entire fretboard. Combining other patterns you know and those on pages 29–39 with these scale forms will enable you to improvise throughout the fretboard in a very systematic manner.

The repetitive cells within the scale forms are connected.

IONIAN

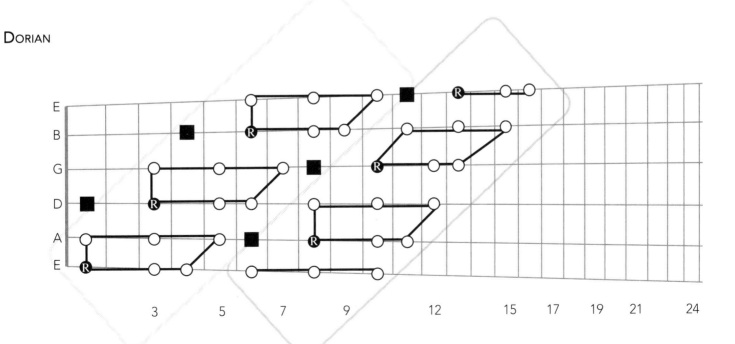

DORIAN

Phrygian

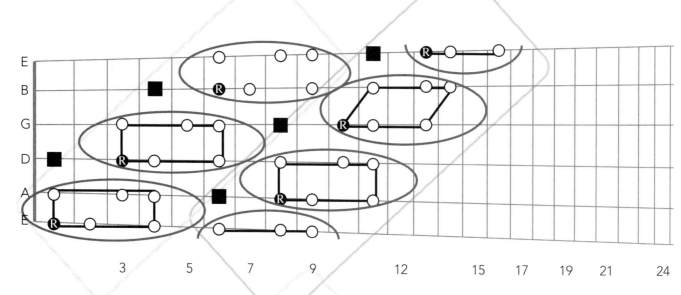

Lydian

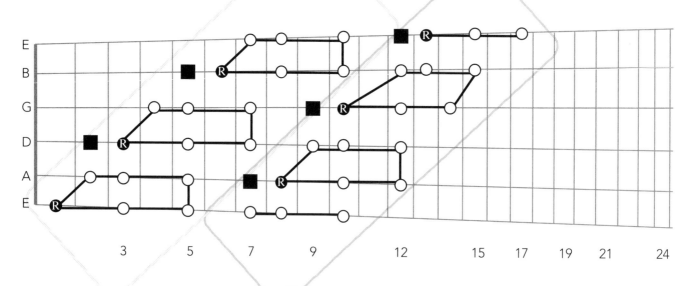

Mixolydian

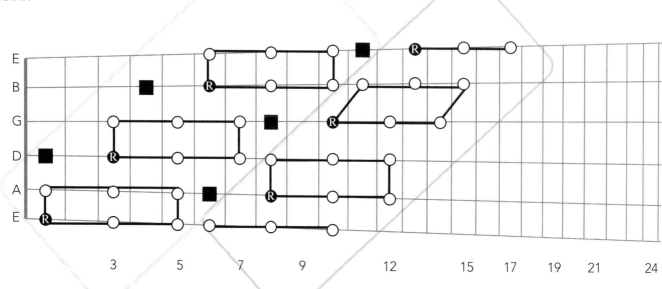

AEOLIAN

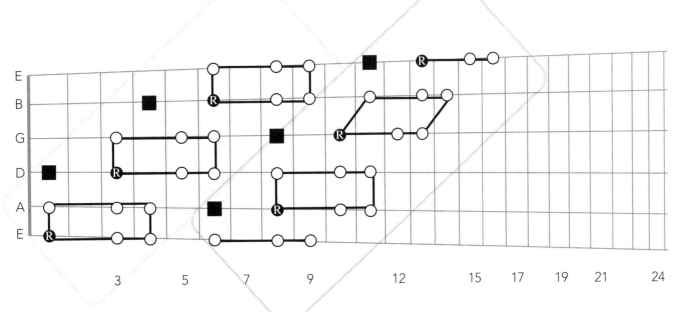

LOCRIAN

HARMONIC MINOR REPETITIVE SCALE FORMS— VERSIONS ONE AND TWO

TCG 50

ETCG 52

Raising the 7th degree of the Aeolian mode (or natural minor scale) one half step creates the harmonic minor scale.

This scale is commonly used in classical, rock, jazz and some ethnic music. The raised 7th creates an augmented 2nd interval (three half steps) between the 6th and 7th degrees, giving it a more exotic sound than many modes and scales.

Theory Nugget

The harmonic minor scale formula is 1–2–♭3–4–5–♭6–7. The half steps are between 2–3, 5–6 and 7–8(1).

Here is the F Harmonic Minor scale on the fretboard. Notice that there is a repetitive scale cell (connected notes) and that in the second scale form (darker gray rectangle), it is adjusted on the 2nd string and has partial pattern on the 1st and 6th strings.

HARMONIC MINOR

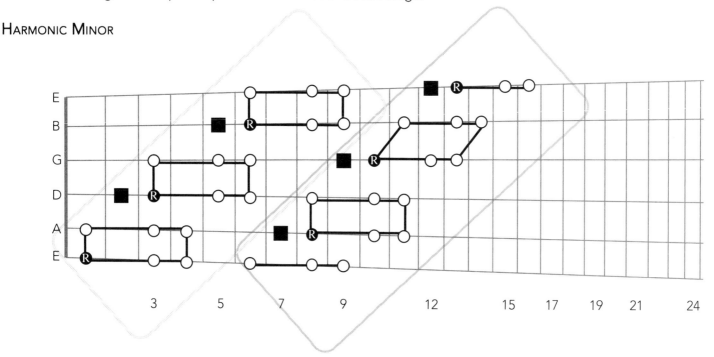

The harmonic minor scale can be used instead of the Aeolian mode but you will need to experiment with it due to its unusual sound.

Try playing A Harmonic Minor over the following Latin progression. Start the scale form on the 5th fret to play in A. Some of the highest notes may not fit on your guitar's fretboard, and therefore need to be transposed down an octave or two.

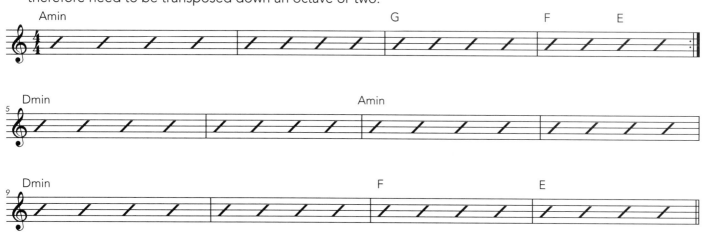

MELODIC MINOR REPETATIVE SCALE FORM

TCG 51

ETCG 57

Raising the 6th and the 7th degree of the Aeolian mode produces the melodic minor scale. Another way of viewing or creating this scale is to lower the 3rd degree of a major scale. This scale is mostly utilized in jazz and sometimes referred to as the *jazz minor* scale. The traditional or classical way of using this scale is to ascend in melodic minor and descend in natural minor (Aeolian).

Try playing this scale as a substitute for Dorian or natural minor. Again, you will need to let your ear be the judge of where it fits best.

Theory Nugget

The melodic minor formula is 1–2–♭3–4–5–6–7. The half steps are between 2–3, and 7–8(1).

F Melodic Minor (ascending form)

17

Here is the melodic minor scale on the fretboard. As with the harmonic minor scale, there is a repetitive scale cell (connected notes) and in the second scale form (darker gray rectangle), it is adjusted on the 2nd string and partial on the 1st and 6th strings.

MELODIC MINOR

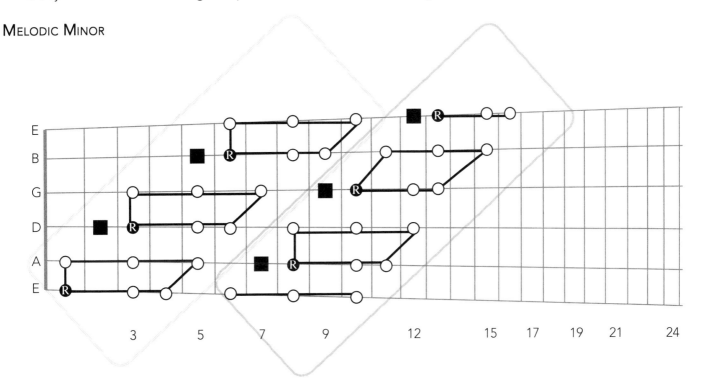

You can use C Melodic Minor over the following chord progression. Transpose this scale form to C by starting it on the 8th fret. You may need to transpose some of it down an octave or two.

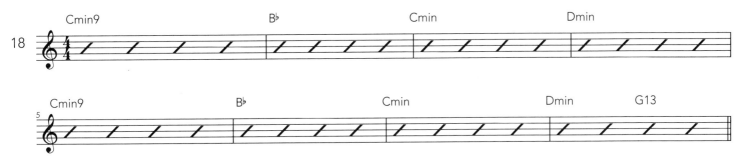

USING MODES AND SCALES

To apply modes and scales to our improvising, we must understand that every chord progression will have a certain character. Certain scales sound better than other scales over certain progressions.

Consider this example progression.

We can play an F Minor Pentatonic scale over this progression, because it is in the key of F Minor. We could also play the F Dorian mode. Either of these scales would be correct. The five-note minor pentatonic scale has a bluesier sound, while the Dorian is jazzier and offers more note choices (seven rather then five). If we were to try to play in F Locrian, our ear would automatically tell us that scale would be incorrect because the ♭5 of the scale would clash with the notes of the chords.

Now, check out this blues progression.

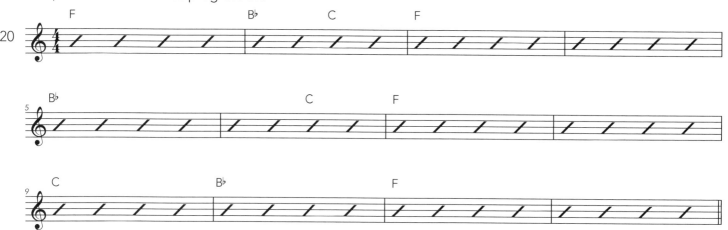

Even though it is in F Major instead of F Minor, we can still use an F Minor Pentatonic scale to solo over this progression. We are used to hearing the ♭3 and ♭7 over major chords in the blues, even though they clash with the notes of the chords, and think of them as "blue notes." The way you determine which scale or mode to use has a lot to do with what your ear tells you, not just your understanding of theory.

Always start by looking at the overall progression. In this case, you should be able to determine fairly quickly that this is a 12-bar blues (see page 82 in *Theory for the Contemporary Guitarist*). The next step would be to look at the first chord, which in this case is F, which usually means you can play some type of F scale. In most blues tunes you can play a minor and/or major pentatonic scale or the Mixolydian mode.

Keep in mind that not every single note in the "correct" scale for a progression will always sound correct. As you play the scale over the progression, you will hear that the majority of the notes do work, while others are only used as *passing tones* (a non-chord tone used between two chord tones in a melody).

It takes some practice, but after a while it will become easier to know which scales and modes to use over which progressions. Listen to various artists, such as Pat Martino and Chick Corea, who are examples of great modal players. Select some tunes of theirs to listen to and try to figure out what scales they are playing.

You don't always need to solo using just one scale. You can alternate between scales. For example, over the progression in example 20 on page 46, you can start with F Minor Pentatonic and then go into F Mixolydian. You can also slip into F Dorian. This gives you many more options to choose from and allows you to be more creative. Experiment.

Remember that some songs *modulate* (the key center changes, see *Theory for the Contemporary Guitarist*, page 87) and you will need to change your scales to fit each new key.

CONCLUSIONS AND REVIEW:

1. A mode is simply a reordering of a scale, and each one has a distinct character and creates a specific mood. There are two ways of viewing or creating the modes: the derivative approach and the parallel approach.

2. The major modes, from brightest to least bright, are: Lydian, Ionian and Mixolydian (which is really a dominant mode). The minor modes, from darkest to least dark, are: Locrian, Phrygian, Aeolian and Dorian.

3. Repetitive Scale Forms Versions One and Two allow you to systematically memorize and master modes and scales quickly, as well as cover a large range of the fretboard.

4. Practicing modes that are almost identical help in developing your ear to hear the subtle differences that exist between them. Practicing the scales we have covered in the following order will help:

   a. Ionian/Lydian/Mixolydian
   b. Dorian/melodic minor
   c. Aeolian/harmonic minor
   d. Phrygian/Locrian

er 5—Chords

ales and modes, the number of chords to be learned seems infinite. Most players simply learn a few chords and stick with them, only venturing out to new chords when necessary. But in the same way that discovering repetitive scale cells speeds up our ability to memorize scales and modes, unveiling repetitive chord patterns will allow you to quickly memorize many more chords. Many chord forms that seem unrelated to each other are exactly the same, with the exact same formulas, but fingering adjustments made for the 2nd string alter their appearance. Repetitive patterns allow for the systematic catagorizing of chords, allowing for easier mastery of the fretboard.

POWER CHORDS

Power chords, also known as *5 chords*, are essential to the sound of much rock music. Widely used in rock, hard rock and alternative music, they have a very bassy/gutsy sound. This is due to the simple formula (root–5–root) and the fact that they are normally played on the lower strings.

THE MOST COMMON POWER CHORDS

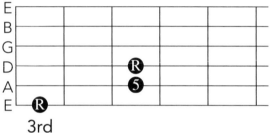

3rd

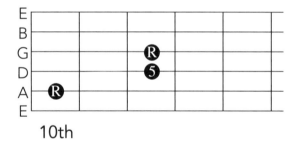

10th

5th

⟶ = An adjustment made to the pattern for the tuning of the 2nd string.

As you can see, the first two chords look identical but are played on different strings. The only difference in the third power chord is that the note on the 2nd string is raised one fret to compensate for the tuning.

REPETITIVE CHORD PATTERNS

TCG 29–32
ETCG 20–21

We will now examine the following chord patterns that appear throughout the neck.

MAJOR TRIADS

Let's first take a look at a simple major triad.

R–5–R–3 Chord Pattern String Set 1

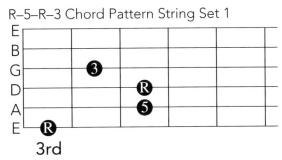

3rd

The formula for this triad is R–3–5 (R=root), but in this chord form it is *voiced* (arranged), from the bottom note up, R–5–R–3. From now on we will treat this voicing, R–5–R–3, as a chord pattern and use it as a point of departure for creating other patterns, as we did with scales.

Let's locate the root on the 5th string then duplicate the R–5–R–3 pattern.

R–5–R–3 Chord Pattern String Set 2

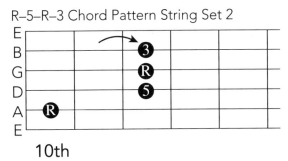

10th

This chord is exactly the same as the previous one, except that we had to raise the top note one fret to adjust for the tuning of the 2nd string. If you are already familiar with this chord form, you may have already made the connection that they are exactly the same chord with the same chord formula and that it only appears to be a different version of the chord because of the tuning of the 2nd string.

Now let's use the same chord pattern starting on the 4th string.

R–5–R–3 Chord Pattern String Set 3

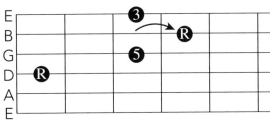

5th

The chord pattern is exactly the same as in the two chord forms above, but the 2nd string note being adjusted this time is the second root in the pattern. Even though the chord appears totally different than the first, it is exactly the same voicing, with exactly the same formula.

These patterns allow you to easily see that many chord forms are exactly the same patterns with an adjustment for the 2nd string. Once you understand that chords are also patterns that repeat throughout the guitar, you can then group all similar patterns together in order to make memorization quicker and easier.

From now on we will be addressing chords in groups of three. Make sure you learn the formula of each chord. This will enable you to easily see the pattern that is repeated throughout the fretboard. In order for you to understand this chapter, it is vitally important for you to understand that the chords in each group all have the same chord pattern that repeats itself on different strings.

CHORD PATTERNS—VERSION ONE

All of the chords we will be examining can be transposed to any key by moving the root to the desired note.

Practice these chords in all keys, playing each string individually, so you can hear each tone and the character it brings to the overall sound of the chord. This is great for ear training as well as helping you memorize the chord formula.

Let's take a look at the simple major triad chord pattern we learned on page 49, this time viewing all three string sets together.

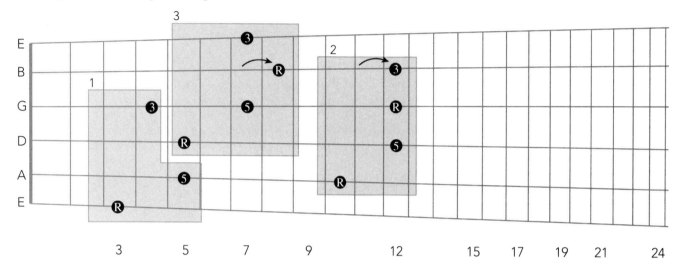

Playing these three chord forms in their numerical sequence—1, 2 and then 3—will enable you to see its evolution from one to the other over a wide range of the fretboard (from the 3rd to the 12th fret). The top 3rd is raised on String Set 2 and the second root in the pattern is raised on String Set 3 because of the 2nd string tuning.

The **Theory Nuggets** in this part of the book provide the chord formulas. In order to play the chords on the guitar, we often change the order of the formula to create a different voicing, or even *invert* them (see pages 32 and 41 in *Theory for the Contemporary Guitarist* for discussions regarding chord inversions).

TCG 37, 58

ETCG 32–34

The following sequence starts with the same major chord pattern (R–5–R–3) only now we will create new closely-related chord types by adjusting the chord forms to fit the new formulas.

Altering the Root in Major and Dominant Chords

In this first diagram, the chord pattern on String Set #1 is adjusted to become a major 7th chord (Maj7), then a dominant 7th (7) and finally a major 6th (6) chord by changing the second root in the pattern, which is on the 4th string of this string set. This creates a sequence of chord patterns: R–5–R–3, R–5–7–3, R–5–♭7–3 and R–5–6–3. Play through them in that order.

Theory Nugget	
Major:	R–3–5
Major 7:	R–3–5–7
Dominant 7:	R–3–5–♭7
Major 6:	R–3–5–6

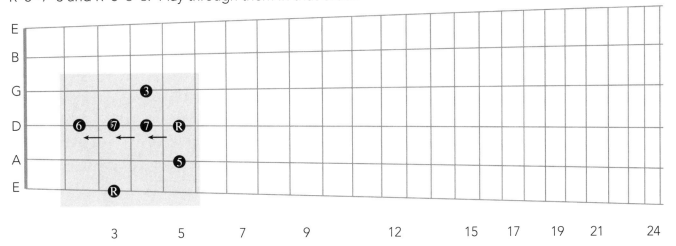

We will now take this chord pattern sequences on String Sets 2 and 3.

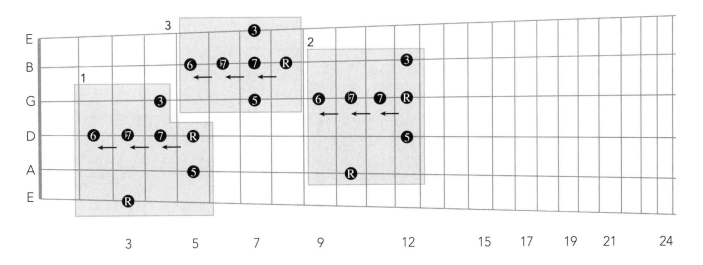

Practicing this sequence of four closely related chord patterns on all three string sets will teach you 12 different chord forms.

This may seem a little tedious at first, but once you grasp the flow of the formulas and the evolution of the sequences from String Sets 1, 2 and 3, your time spent in memorizing chords will shorten tremendously. You will also acquire an all-inclusive view of how similar chords are distributed throughout the fretboard.

ALTERING THE 5TH IN MAJOR 7TH CHORDS

TCG 37

ETCG 32

Let's take a look at the 5th of a major 7th chord and see what chords are created by altering that tone. We will use the chord pattern for the major 7th chord we arrived at on page 51: R–5–7–3.

The first chord we will play is a major 7♯5 (Maj7♯5). We arrive at this chord by raising the 5th in our chord pattern. Starting there and following the arrow to lower the 5th, we return to the regular major 7th chord. Lowering the 5th again gets us a major 7♭5 (Maj7♭5). If we apply this chord pattern sequence to String Sets 1, 2 and 3, we arrive at nine chord forms in total.

Theory Nugget

Major 7♯5: R–3–♯5–7
Major 7♭5: R–3–♭5–7

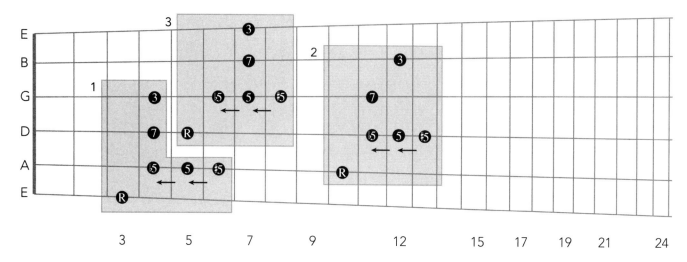

ALTERING THE 3RD IN THE MAJOR CHORD

Altering the 3rd in the R–5–R–3 chord pattern also changes the chord family: our major chord becomes minor (min). We also create a suspended 4 chord (sus4), where the 3rd is replaced by a 4th.

Theory Nugget

Suspended 4: R–4–5
Minor: R–♭3–5

Start by rasing the 3rd to the 4th to create the sus4. If we lower the 4th back down to the 3rd, we return to the major chord. Lowering the 3rd again creates a minor chord. Again, if we apply this chord pattern sequence to String Sets 1, 2 and 3, we arrive at nine chord forms in total.

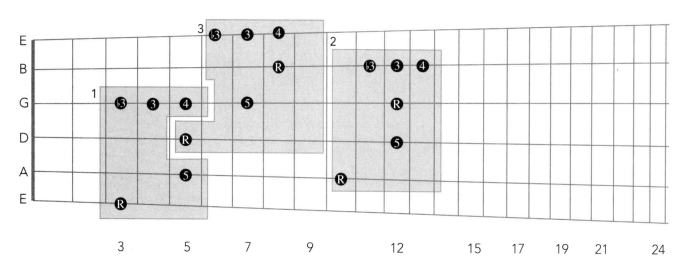

ALTERING THE 3RD IN DOMINANT 7TH CHORDS

Since there are many types of dominant 7th chords, we will begin taking a look at them by altering the 3rd in the dominant 7th chord pattern we discovered on page 51: R–3–5–♭7. As a result, we'll discover chord forms for suspended 7th (sus7), minor 7th (min7) chords, and an additional alteration to the 5th will give us a minor 7♭5 (min7♭5) chord.

Let's start by raising the 3rd in the chord pattern to create a sus7 chord. It differs from the sus4 chord in that the ♭7 replaces one of the roots in the chord pattern. Dropping the 4th down to the 3rd gives us the dominant 7th chord and then dropping it again gives us a min7. We have the option of doing an additional alteration, this time lowering the 5th (in parentheses), to give us the popular jazz chord, min7♭5. Be sure to include the min7♭5 in the chord pattern sequence on all three string sets.

<table>
<tr><td>TCG 37</td></tr>
<tr><td>ETCG 33</td></tr>
</table>

Theory Nugget

Suspended 7:	R–4–5–♭7
Minor 7:	R–♭3–5–♭7
Minor 7♭5:	R–♭3–♭5–♭7

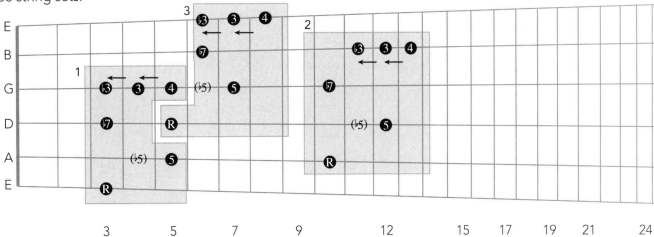

ALTERING THE 5TH IN DOMINANT 7TH CHORDS

If we start by raising the 5th in the dominant 7th chord pattern we get a dominant 7♯5 chord (7♯5). When we lower the 5th we return to a dominant 7th chord and lowering it again gets us a dominant 7♭5 chord (7♭5). You also have the option of lowering the 3rd to ♭3 (in parentheses) to create min7♭5 chords (R–♭3–♭5–♭7).

<table>
<tr><td>TCG 73</td></tr>
<tr><td>ETCG 86–87</td></tr>
</table>

Theory Nugget

Dominant 7♯5: R–3–♯5–♭7
Dominant 7♭5: R–3–♭5–♭7

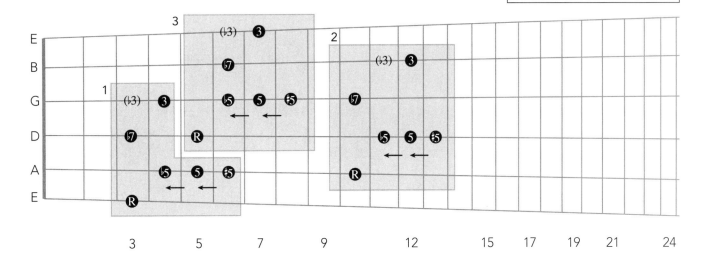

CHORD PATTERNS FOR EXTENDED CHORDS

TCG 73

ETCG 87–88

ALTERING THE 9TH IN A DOMINANT CHORD

Slightly changing the basic chord pattern by dropping the 5th and putting the 3rd just above the root allows us to include the 9th. The 9th is a *compound* version of a 2nd (a 2nd plus an octave). Chords that include compound intervals are called *extended chords* (see page 58 of *Theory for the Contemporary Guitarist*).

Chords such as these, where there are more notes than fingers, typically have the 5th omitted. This does not affect the character of the chord, since the 3rd and 7th provide the basic flavor (major, minor or dominant). The omitted notes are gray in the formulas in the Theory Nuggets. This omission is a variation on Version One of the Chord Pattern.

Let's start by raising the 9th to create a dominant #9 chord (7#9). Lowering the #9 gets us a dominant 9th chord (9) and lowering again gets us the dominant ♭9 (7♭9). As always, do this on all three string sets to learn nine different chord forms.

Theory Nugget

Dominant #9: R–3–5–♭7–#9
Dominant 9: R–3–5–♭7–9
Dominant ♭9: R–3–5–♭7–♭9

5 = From now on, a gray chord tone in any Theory Nugget is a tone not included in the voicing.

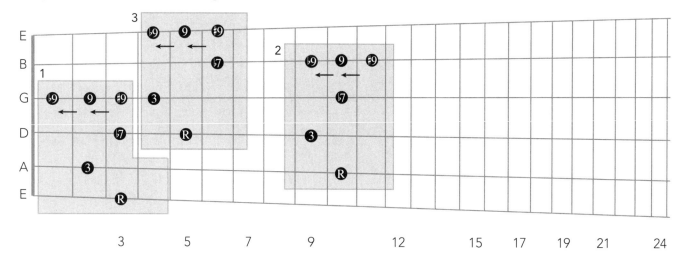

ALTERING THE 3RD AND 7TH IN 9TH CHORDS

Altering the 3rd and the 7th in 9th chords reveals two other popular chord forms. Start with the 9th and the 7th in the natural positions for the major 9th chord (Maj9). For the minor 9th chord (min9), lower the 7th and the 3rd. As we saw above, lowering just the 7th creates the dominant 9th chord.

TCG 59

ETCG 69

Theory Nugget

Major 9:   R–3–5–7–9
Dominant 9: R–3–5–♭7–9
Minor 9:   R–♭3–5–♭7–9

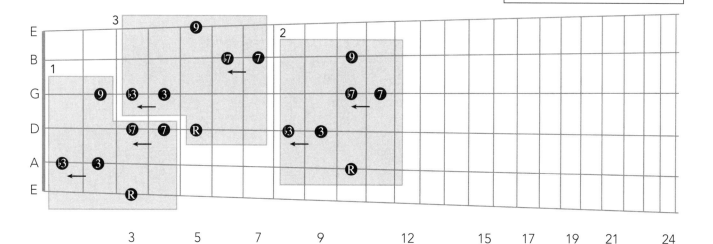

ALTERING THE 3RD IN 11TH CHORDS

An 11th is the compound version of a 4th (a 4th plus an octave). The most commonly used 11th chords are the dominant 11th (11) and the minor 11th (min11) chords. For 11th chords, we need a new chord pattern: R–11–7–3.

Let's start with a lowered 7th and the 3rd in its natural position to create an 11 chord. From there, simply lower the 3rd to get a min11 chord. The 5th and 9th are typically omitted. Do this on all three string sets to learn nine 11th chord forms.

TCG 59

ETCG 70

Theory Nugget

Dominant 11: R–3–5–♭7–9–11

Minor 11:   R–♭3–5–♭7–9–11

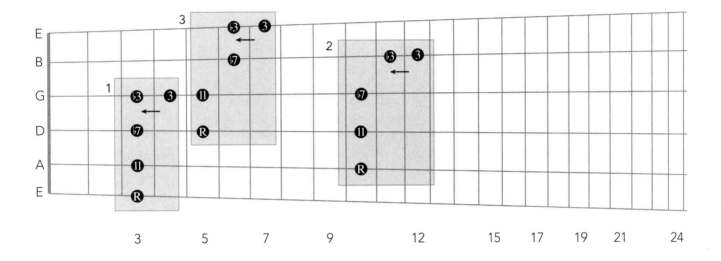

13TH CHORDS

For the following 13th chords we will not be using the root. We will also omit the 5th and the 11th which are also optional for this chord. The chord pattern is 7–3–13–9. The 13th is just a compound interval of a 6th, but when the 7th is present in the chord, it is thought of as a 13th, regardless of the voicing.

Rootless voicings sound best when played with a bass player or other bass instrument playing the root. This chord pattern will need to be used with discretion when playing with bass instruments since the 7th on the bass strings of the guitar may clash with other low notes.

Start with the major 13th chord (Maj13) by leaving all of the notes in their natural positions. Then, lower the 7 to ♭7 to create the dominant 13th chord (13). Do this on all three string sets to get six different chord forms.

TCG 60
ETCG 71–72

> **Theory Nugget**
>
> Major 13:   R–3–5–7–9–11–13
> Dominant 13: R–3–5–♭7–9–11–13

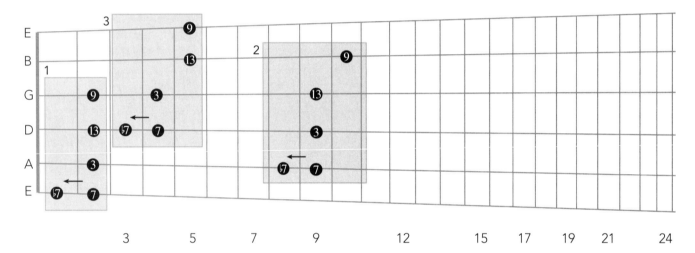

The following are the minor 13th (min13) and the suspended 13th (sus13) chords. The minor 13th is like the dominant 13th, but it also has a lowered 3rd.

Begin by raising the 3rd in the 7–3–13–9 pattern you learned on page 55 so that it becomes a 4th to create the sus13, then lower it one whole step to make the min13. Doing this on all three strings sets gets you six different chord forms.

> **Theory Nugget**
>
> Minor 13:   R–♭3–5–♭7–9–11–13
> Suspended 13: R–4–5–♭7–9–11–13

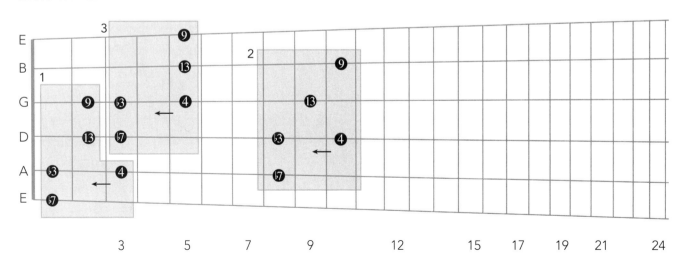

CHORD PATTERNS—VERSION TWO

The 5–R–3–7 chord pattern is an inversion of R–5–7–3 from the 7th chords on pages 52 and 53. Note that even though the inversion is different, the formula for the chords always remains the same. Again, you can find thorough discussions of inversions on pages 31 and 41 of *Theory for the Contemporary Guitarist*.

TCG 32, 41
ETCG 22, 38–39

ALTERING THE ROOT IN MAJOR AND DOMINANT CHORDS

Always play the first chord in the sequence and follow the arrows to create the other chords. This chord pattern sequence starts with the major chord and goes on to reveal chord forms for the Maj7, 7 and Maj6. Playing this on all three string sets teaches you 12 different chord forms.

Theory Nuggets	
Major:	R–3–5
Major 7:	R–3–5–7
Dominant 7:	R–3–5–♭7
Major 6:	R–3–5–6

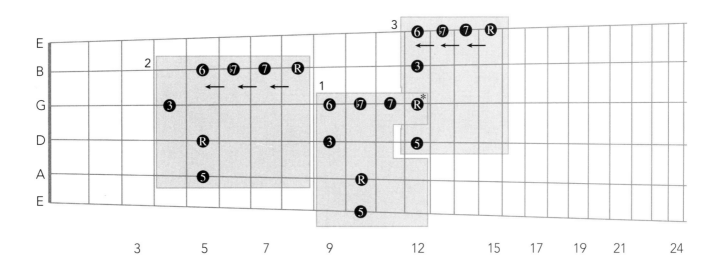

* This root is in both patterns 1 and 3.

ALTERING THE 5TH IN MAJOR 7TH CHORDS

Start by raising the 5th to create the Maj7♯5, then lower it one step at a time to get the Maj7 and Maj7♭5.

TCG 37, 64
ETCG 33, 75

Theory Nugget

Major 7♯5: R–3–♯5–7
Major 7: R–3–5–7
Major 7♭5: R–3–♭5–7

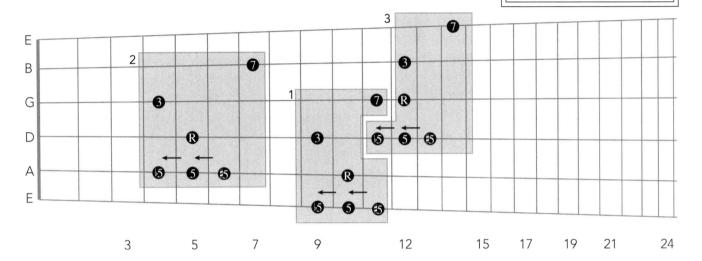

ALTERING THE 3RD IN THE MAJOR CHORD

Start by raising the 3rd to create the sus4, then lower it one step at a time to create the major and the minor chords.

TCG 62
ETCG 74

Theory Nugget

Suspended 4: R–4–5
Major: R–3–5
Minor: R–♭3–5

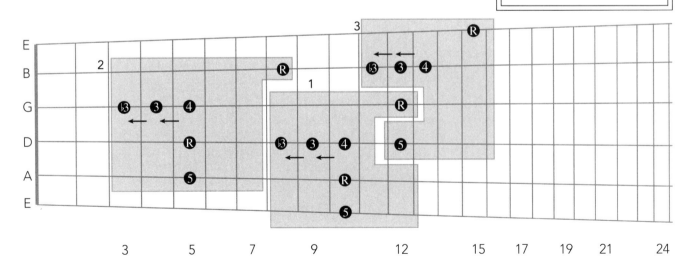

ALTERING THE 3RD IN 7TH CHORDS

Start by raising the 3rd to create the sus7, then lower it one step at a time to create the 7 and min7 chords.

TCG 37

ETCG 32–33

Theory Nugget

Suspended 7: R–4–5–♭7
Dominant 7:   R–3–5–♭7
Minor 7:   R–♭3–5–♭7

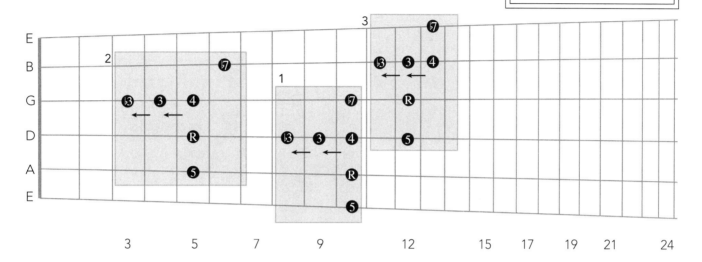

ALTERING THE 5TH IN DOMINANT 7TH CHORDS

Start by rasing the 5th to create the 7♯5, then lower it one step at a time to get the 7 and 7♭5.

TCG 73

ETCG 86–87

Theory Nugget

Dominant 7♯5: R–3–♯5–♭7
Dominant 7:   R–3–5–♭7
Dominant 7♭5: R–♭3–♭5–♭7

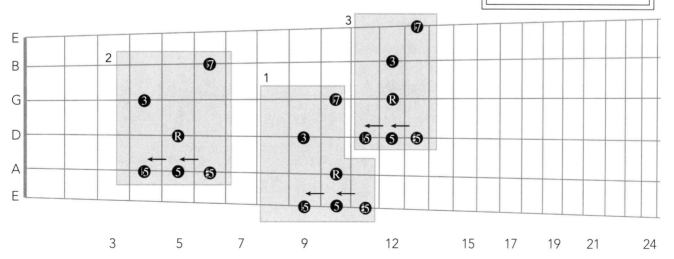

ALTERING THE 9TH IN DOMINANT CHORDS

The chord pattern in this sequence is 3–7–R–9. The three chord types in this diagram are all dominant, so the 7 will be ♭7. Start with the 9 raised to create a 7♯9. Then lower it one step at a time to create the 9 and 7♭9 chords. Doing this on all three string sets yields nine different chord forms.

TCG 73

ETCG 87

Theory Nugget

Major ♯9:   R–3–5–♭7–♯9
Dominant 9: R–3–5–♭7–9
Dominant ♭9: R–3–5–♭7–♭9

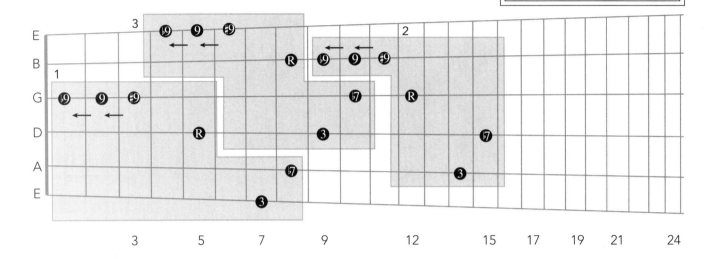

Some of these chords are more difficult to play in the lower positions. Chord Pattern 1 in the diagram above is a good example of this. Such chord patterns, however, are very useful because they create more unique or unusual-sounding chords.

ALTERING THE 3RD AND 7TH IN 9TH CHORDS

Continuing with the 3–7–R–9 chord pattern, we will start with the 7th and 9th in their natural positions for a Maj9 chord. Lower the 7th to create the 9 chord and then the 3rd to create a min9.

TCG 59

ETCG 69–70

Theory Nugget

Major 9:   R–3–5–7–9
Dominant 9: R–3–5–♭7–9
Minor 9:   R–♭3–5–♭7–9

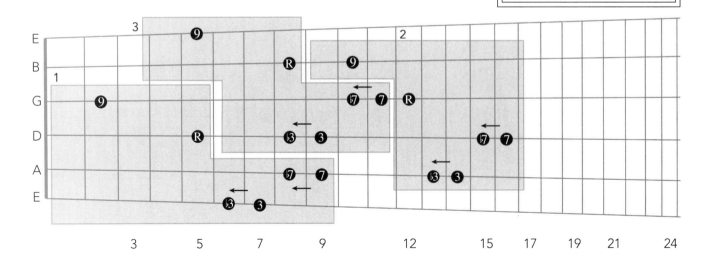

ALTERING THE 3RD IN 11TH CHORDS

The chord pattern here is 11–R–3–7. We will look at the 11 and min11 chords, so the 7s will be ♭7. Start with the 3rd in the natural position for the 11 chord and then lower it to create the min11. Done on all three string sets, this yields six different chord forms.

TCG 59
ETCG 70–71

Theory Nuggets

Dominant 11: R–3–5–♭7–9–11
Minor 11:   R–♭3–5–♭7–9–11

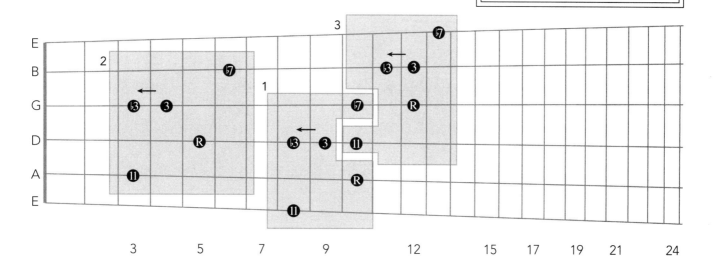

13TH CHORDS

Using a 3–7–9–13 rootless chord pattern, we will learn Maj13 and dominant 13 chord forms. See the 13th Chord section on page 56 for a discussion of playing rootless voicings. Start with the 7th in the natural position for a Maj13 and then lower it to create the 13 chord.

TCG 60

ETCG 71–72

Theory Nugget

Major 13:   R–3–5–7–9–11–13
Dominant 13: R–3–5–♭7–9–11–13

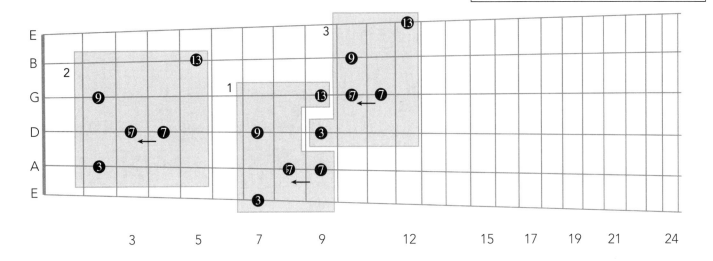

We'll now use the 3–7–9–13 chord pattern to create sus13 and min13 chord forms. Start with the 3rd raised to create the sus13, and then lower it a whole step to get the min13.

TCG 60

ETCG 72

Theory Nugget

Suspended 13: R–4–5–♭7–9–11–13
Minor 13:   R–♭3–5–♭7–9–11–13

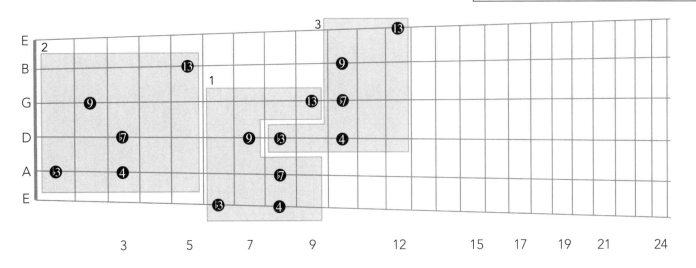

CHORD PATTERNS—VERSION THREE

Some of the chord forms in this version of the chord patterns require quite a stretch, so you will need to practice reaching them. For hard to reach chords, always finger the note closest to the bridge of the guitar first, regardless of which string it is on. Remember that all of these chord patterns are transposable to any root by simply moving the root to the desired note.

TCG 37, 39, 41, 58

ETCG 32–33, 38, 68

ALTERING THE ROOT IN MAJOR AND DOMINANT CHORDS

This chord pattern is 3–R–R–5. Remember to play the first chord in the sequence and follow the arrows through it in order to create the other chords. Start with all of the notes in their natural positions for a major chord and then lower the first root in the pattern one step at a time to create the Maj7, 7 and 6 chords. Doing this on all three string sets reveals 12 different chord forms.

Theory Nugget

Major: R–3–5
Major 7:   R–3–5–7
Dominant 7: R–3–5–♭7
Major 6:   R–3–5–6

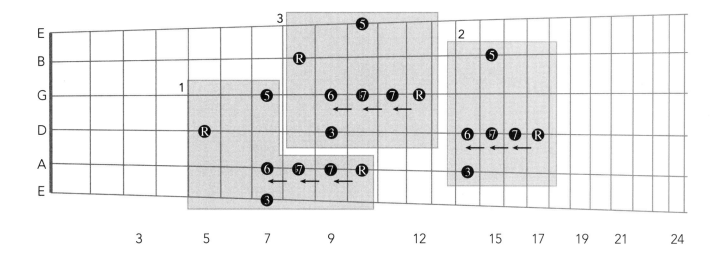

ALTERING THE 5TH IN MAJOR 7TH CHORDS

Using a 3–7–R–5 chord pattern, we will find Maj7♯5, Maj7 and Maj7♭5 chord forms by altering the 5th. Start with the 5th raised for the Maj7♯5, then lower it one step at a time to get the Maj7 and Maj7♭5 chords.

TCG 37, 64

ETCG 33

Theory Nugget

Major 7♯5:   R–3–♯5–7
Major 7:   R–3–5–7
Major 7♭5:   R–3–♭5–7

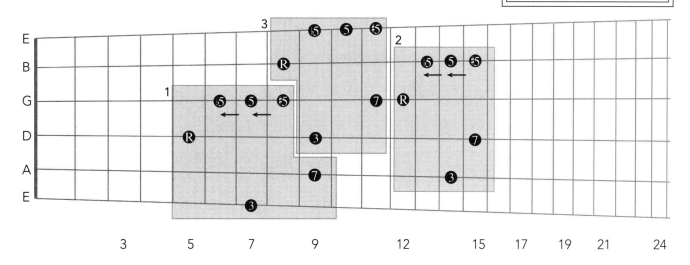

ALTERING THE 3RD IN THE MAJOR CHORD

The chord pattern here is 3–R–R–5 and we will be altering the 3rd to find sus4, major and minor chord forms. Start with the 3rd raised to get the sus4, and then step down through the sequence to find the major and minor chords.

TCG 29–32, 62

ETCG 20, 62

Theory Nugget

Suspended 4:	R–4–5
Major:	R–3–5
Minor:	R–♭3–5

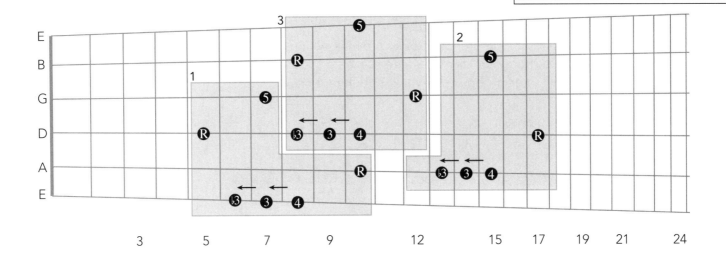

ALTERING THE 3RD IN 7TH CHORDS

In this 3–7–R–5 chord pattern, we will find dominant and minor 7 chord forms by altering the 3rd, and all of the 7s are ♭7. Start with the 3rd raised for the sus7 and then step down to the 7 and min7 chords.

TCG 37

ETCG 32–33

Theory Nugget

Suspended 7:	R–4–5–♭7
Dominant 7:	R–3–5–♭7
Minor 7:	R–♭3–5–♭7

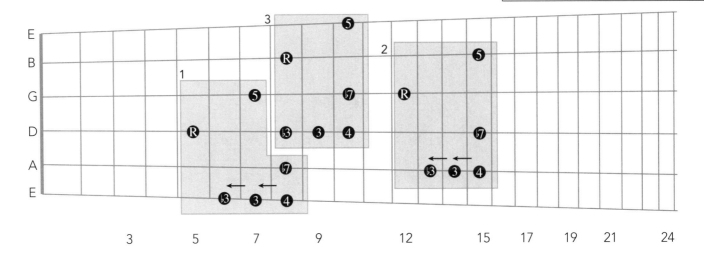

ALTERING THE 5TH IN DOMINANT 7TH CHORDS

This chord pattern is 3–7–R–5 and we will be altering the 5th to find 7#5, 7 and 7♭5 chord forms. All of the 7s are ♭7. Start with the 5th raised for the 7#5, then lower it one step at a time to get the 7 and then 7♭5 chords. As always, do this on all three string sets.

TCG 43, 73

ETCG 33, 38–39, 86–87

Theory Nuggets

Dominant 7#5: R–3–#5–♭7
Dominant 7:   R–3–5–♭7
Dominant 7♭5: R–3–♭5–♭7

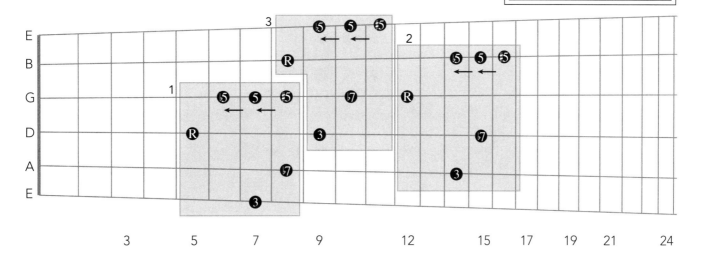

ALTERING THE 9TH IN DOMINANT CHORDS

With this 9–7–R–3 chord pattern, the 7s are all ♭7 and we will alter the 9th to find 7#9, 9 and 7♭9 chord forms. Start with the 9th raised for the 7#9 and then follow the sequence, lowering the 9th one step at a time to get the 9 and 7♭9 chord forms.

TCG 73

ETCG 87–88

Theory Nugget

Dominant #9: R–3–5–♭7–#9
Dominant 9: R–3–5–♭7–9
Dominant ♭9: R–3–5–♭7–♭9

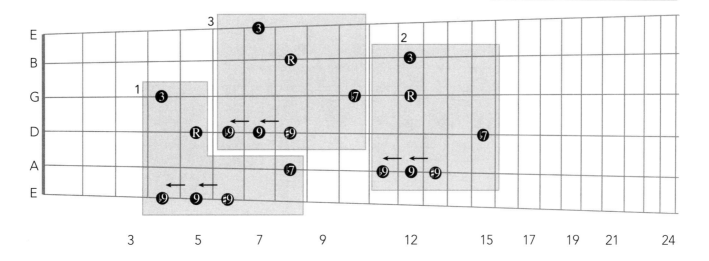

ALTERING THE 3RD AND 7TH IN 9TH CHORDS

This is a 9–7–R–3 chord pattern and will use it for Maj9 and min9 chord forms. Start with the 3rd and the 7th in their natural positions for the Maj9 and then lower them both to create the min9.

TCG 59

ETCG 69

Theory Nuggets

Major 9: R–3–5–7–9

Minor 9: R–$\flat$3–5–$\flat$7–9

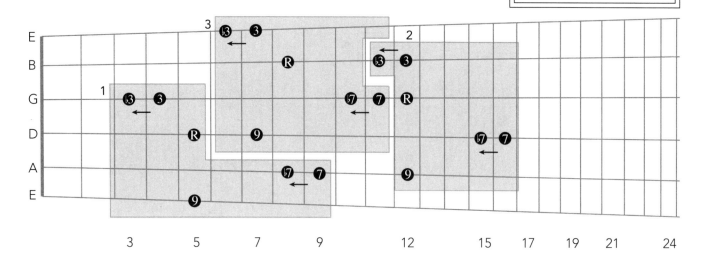

ALTERING THE 3RD IN 11TH CHORDS

This rootless chord pattern is 9–3–7–11. Use it to learn dominant 11 and min11 chord forms. Start with a $\flat$7 and a 3 in the natural position for the dominant 11 and then lower the 3rd for the min11.

TCG 59

ETCG 70–71

Theory Nuggets

Dominant 11: R– 3–5– $\flat$7–9–11

Minor 11:   R–$\flat$3–5–$\flat$7–9–11

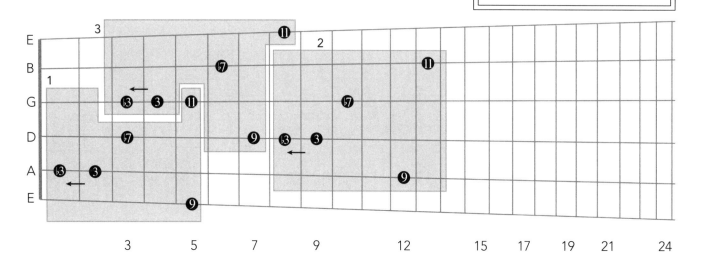

13TH CHORDS

We'll use this 7–9–3–13 rootless chord pattern to find Maj13 and dominant 13 chord forms by altering the 7th . Start with the 7th in its natural position for the Maj13 and then lower it to create a dominant 13.

TCG 60

ETCG 71

Theory Nugget

Major 13:   R–3–5–7–9–11–13

Dominant 13: R–3–5–$\flat$7–9–11–13

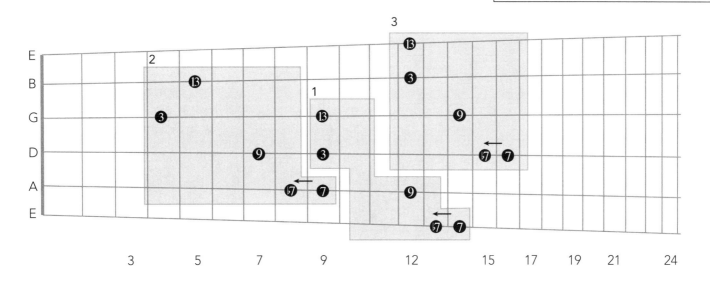

The 7–9–3–13 chord pattern will reveal sus13 and min13 chord forms. Start with the 7th lowered and the 3rd raised for the sus13, and then move down a whole step from the 4th for the min13.

TCG 60

ETCG 72

Theory Nugget

Suspended 13: R–4–5–$\flat$7–9–11–13

Minor 13:   R–$\flat$3–5–$\flat$7–9–11–13

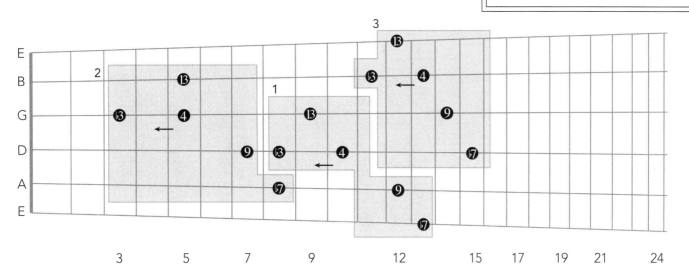

CHORD PATTERNS—VERSION FOUR

Version Four, which offers some interesting inversions of the chord patterns, will be our last chord pattern version.

ALTERING THE ROOT IN MAJOR AND DOMINANT CHORDS

The order of chord forms in this R–3–5–R sequence is major, maj7, dominant 7th and 6. Start with all of the notes in their natural positions and then lower the root one step at a time to reveal the other chord forms.

> TCG 37, 41, 58
> ETCG 32–33,
> 37–38, 68

> **Theory Nugget**
> Major: R–3–5
> Major 7:   R–3–5–7
> Dominant 7:   R–3–5–♭7
> Major 6:   R–3–5–6

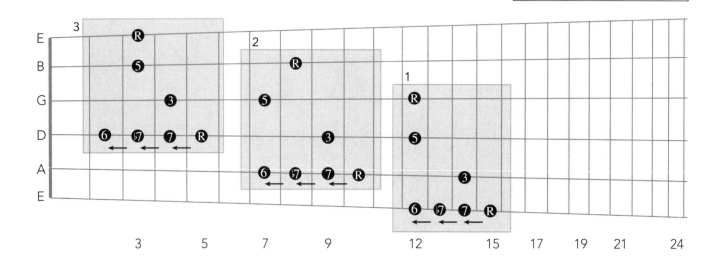

ALTERING THE 5TH IN MAJOR 7TH CHORDS

We will use this 7–3–5–R chord pattern to reveal chord forms for the Maj7♯5, Maj7 and Maj7♭5 by altering the 5th. Start with the 5th raised for Maj7♯5, then lower it one step at a time for the Maj7 and Maj7♭5 chord forms.

> TCG 37, 64
> ETCG 33, 75

> **Theory Nugget**
> Major 7♯5:   R–3–♯5–7
> Major 7:   R–3–5–7
> Major 7♭5:   R–3–♭5–7

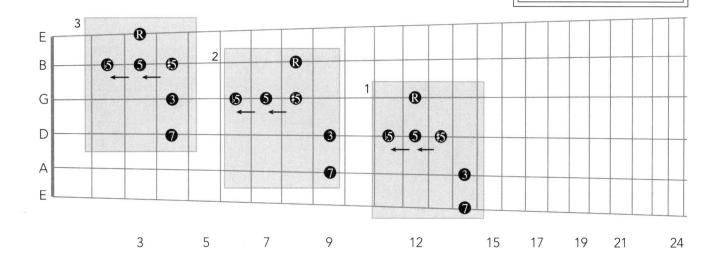

ALTERING THE 3RD IN THE MAJOR CHORD

We'll use this R–3–5–R chord pattern to reveal sus4, major and minor chords by altering the 3rd. Start with the 3rd raised for the sus4 and then lower it step by step for the major and minor chord forms. As always, do this on all three sets and be rewarded with nine different chord forms.

TCG 29–32, 62
ETCG 20, 74

Theory Nugget

Suspended 4: R–4–5
Major: R–3–5
Minor: R–♭3–5

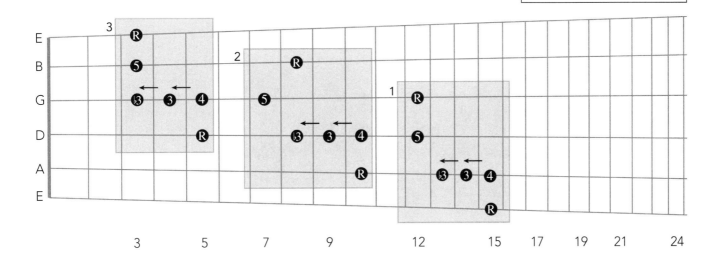

ALTERING THE 3RD IN 7TH CHORDS

This 7–3–5–R chord pattern will reveal sus7, 7 and min7 chord forms. Start with the 3rd raised for the sus4, and follow the sequence, lowering the 4th to the 3rd and then the ♭3rd for the other chord forms.

TCG 37, 41
ETCG 32–39

Theory Nugget

Suspended 7: R–4–5–♭7
Dominant 7: R–3–5–♭7
Minor 7:   R–♭3–5–♭7

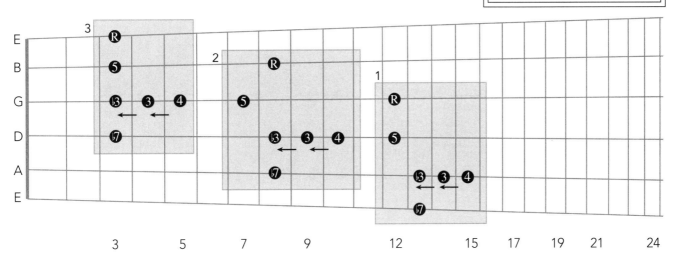

ALTERING THE 5TH IN DOMINANT 7TH CHORDS

In this 7–3–5–R chord pattern, we will alter the 5th to reveal 7$^\sharp$5, 7 and 7$^\flat$5 chord forms. Start with the 7th lowered and the 5th raised for the 7$^\sharp$5 and then lower the 5th one step at a time to find the 7 and 7$^\flat$5 chord forms. Do this on all three string sets to learn nine different chord forms.

TCG 73

ETCG 33, 86–87

Theory Nugget

Dominant $^\sharp$5: R–3–$^\sharp$5–$^\flat$7
Dominant 7: R–3–5–$^\flat$7
Dominant $^\flat$5: R–3–$^\flat$5–$^\flat$7

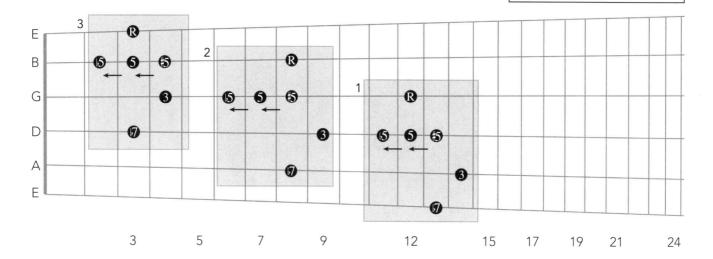

ALTERING THE 9TH IN DOMINANT 9TH CHORDS

This chord pattern is 7–9–3–R. Since these are dominant chords, all of the 7s are $^\flat$7. We will alter the 9th to create 7$^\sharp$9, 9 and 7$^\flat$9 chord forms. Start with the 9th raised for the 7$^\sharp$9 and then lower it one step at a time to create the 9 and 7$^\flat$9 chord forms.

TCG 59, 73

ETCG 70, 87–88

Theory Nugget

Dominant $^\sharp$9: R–3–5–$^\flat$7
Dominant 9: R–$^\flat$3–5–$^\flat$7–9
Dominant $^\flat$9: R– 3–5–$^\flat$7–$^\flat$9

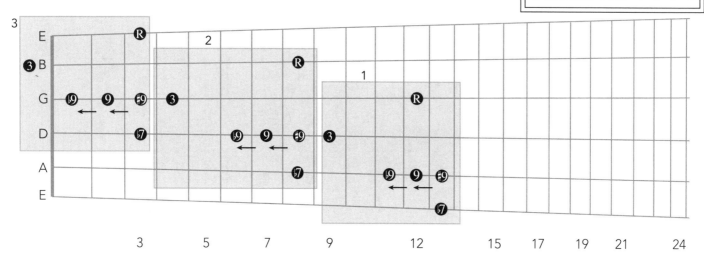

ALTERING THE 3RD AND 7TH IN 9TH CHORDS

We will use a 7–9–3–R chord pattern to find Maj9 and min9 by altering the 3rd and 7th. Start with all of the notes in their natural positions for the Maj9 and then lower the 3rd and the 7th to create a min9.

TCG 59

ETCG 69

Theory Nugget

Major 9: R–3–5–7–9

Minor 9: R–♭3–5–♭7–9

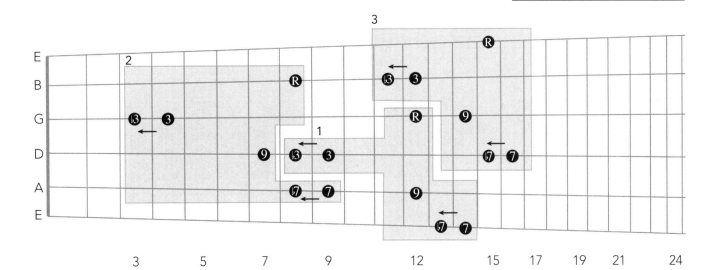

ALTERING THE 3RD IN 11TH CHORDS

This is a 7–3–11–R chord pattern. If we use a lowered 7th and then alter the 3rd, we can find both dominant 11 and min11 chord forms on all three string sets. Start with the 3rd in the natural position for the 11 chord and then lower it for the min11.

TCG 59

ETCG 70–71

Theory Nugget

Dominant 11: R–3–5–♭7–9–11

Minor 11:   R–♭3–5–♭7–9–11

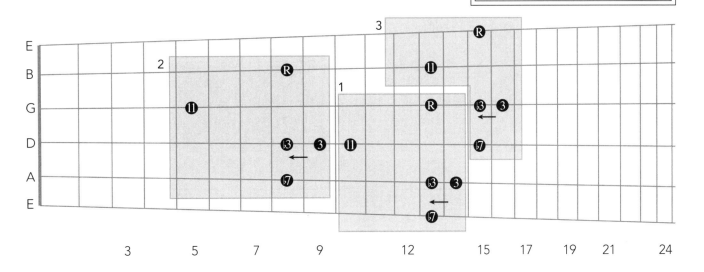

13TH CHORDS

We can lower the 7 of this 13–3–7–9 rootless chord pattern to move from a Maj13 to a dominant 13.

TCG 60

ETCG 71

Theory Nugget

Major 13:   R–3–5–7–9–11–13
Dominant 13:   R–3–5–♭7–9–11–13

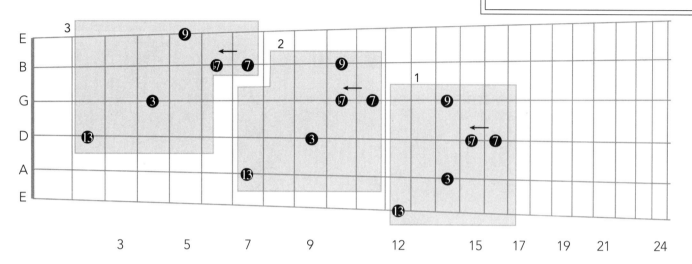

We will use this 13–3–7–9 chord pattern to find sus13 and min13 chord forms by altering the 3rd. Start by lowering the 7th and raising the 3rd to the 4th to make the sus13 and then lower the 3rd a whole step to find the min13 chord form.

TCG 60

ETCG 72

Theory Nugget

Suspended 13: R–4–5–♭7–9–11–13
Minor 13:   R–♭3–5–♭7–9–11–13

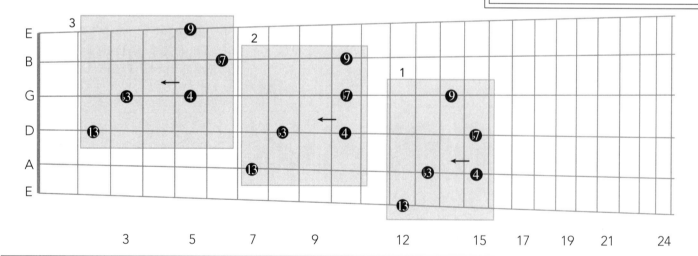

CONCLUSIONS AND REVIEW:

1. Like scales, chords have repetitive patterns that can be transposed anywhere on the fretboard.

2. The repetitive patterns must be adjusted for the 2nd string.

3. Grouping similar patterns and formulas together will enable you to memorize many chord forms more quickly.

4. It is important to memorize the chord formulas.

Chapter 6—Arpeggios

An *arpeggio* is the notes of a chord played one after the other. Many great guitarists use arpeggios while improvising to create interesting melodic lines. Keep in mind that although arpeggios have the same chord formulas as the chords on which they are based, they do not have to be made from the chord forms that you know. The arpeggios we will be studying are played melodically. In other words, they often have more than one note on a single string. There are unique repetitive patterns on the fretboard for each arpeggio type. Studying these patterns will simplify the process of learning arpeggios for the different chord types and using them in your playing.

> The **Theory Nuggets** in this chapter will give the chord formulas for the arpeggios.

REPETITIVE ARPEGGIO PATTERNS

> TCG 29, 32
> ETCG 20, 22, 24

MAJOR

Read these patterns just like the scale diagrams: Start on the lowest note on the lowest string and play up to the highest note on the highest string, from left to right and bottom to top. Also practice them descending, right to left and top to bottom. Remember that these patterns are fully transposable by simply moving the root to the desired note.

> **Theory Nugget**
> Major: R–3–5

Here are two-string G Major repetitive arpeggio patterns on three different string sets: 6–5, 4–3 and 2–1. Notice that the first diagram is root position, the next is 1st inversion and the third is 2nd inversion. The same fingering is used for each three-note group in a diagram.

Root Position

1st Inversion

2nd Inversion

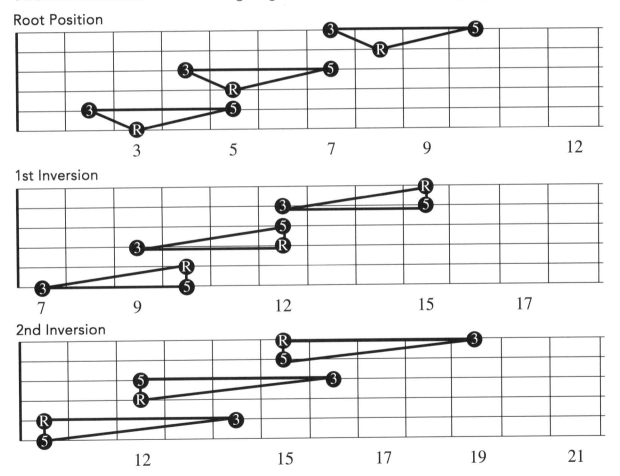

The following exercise will help with better execution of the above G Arpeggio.

MINOR

Here are two-string G Minor repetitive arpeggio patterns on three different string sets: 6–5, 4–3 and 2–1.

TCG 29, 32
ETCG 20, 22, 24

Theory Nugget

Minor: R–♭3–5

Root Position

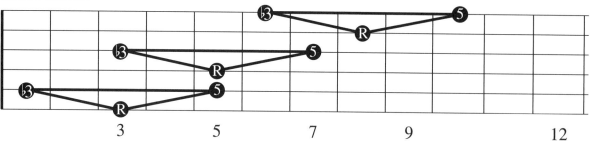

1st Inversion

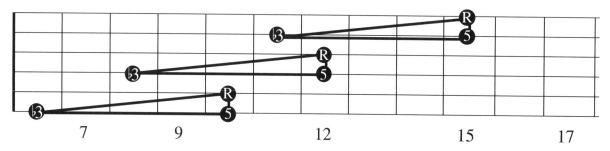

2nd Inversion

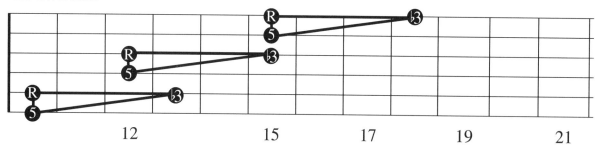

This C Minor arpeggio example has a classical sound. It starts from the top string and works its way down.

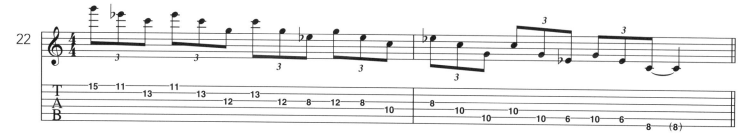

AUGMENTED

Although this isn't a commonly used arpeggio, it has an interesing sound over a passing augmented chord.

TCG 29
ETCG 21, 23, 25

Theory Nugget
Augmented: R–3–#5

Root Position

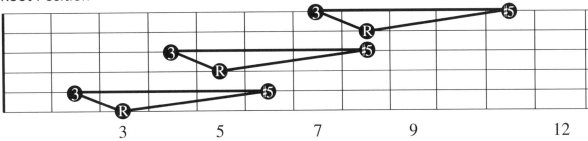

1st Inversion

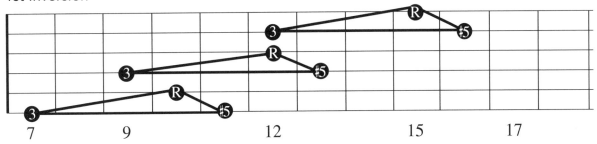

2nd Inversion

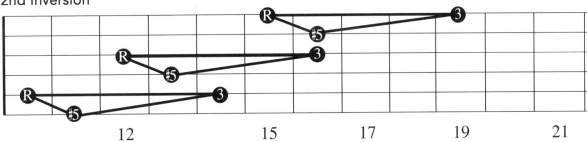

Here is a G Augmented arpeggio passage.

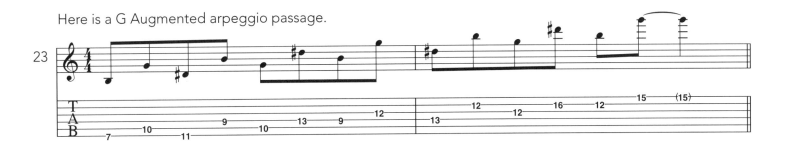

DIMINISHED

Here are two-string G Diminished repetitive arpeggio patterns on the three different string sets: 6–5, 4–3 and 2–1.

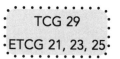

Theory Nuggets
Diminished: R–♭3–♭5

Root Position

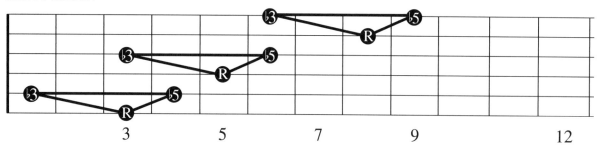

1st Inversion

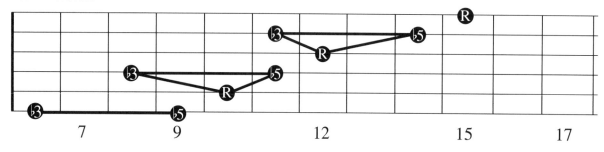

2nd Inversion

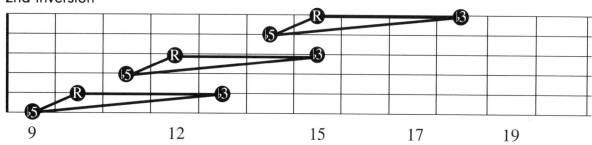

This is an interesting sounding diminished arpeggio exercise in the key of B.

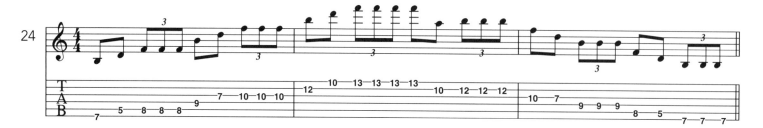

SUSPENDED

Use these over sus4 chords.

TCG 62

ETCG 74

Theory Nuggets

Suspended 4: R–3–4

Root Position

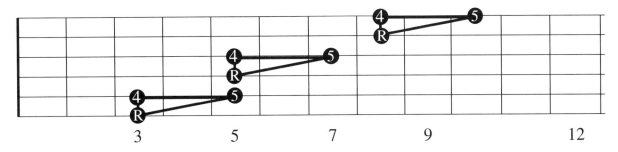

1st Inversion

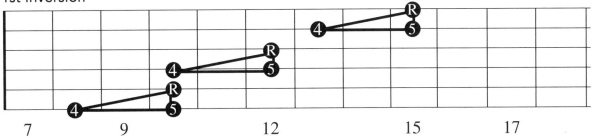

2nd Inversion

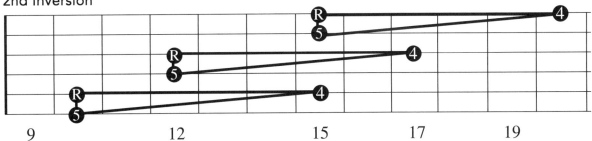

Notice that even though these arpeggiated Asus4 chords are basically smooth sounding, the skips give it a more angular twist.

MAJOR 6

There are four notes in this chord, so there are three inversions of the arpeggio patterns.

TCG 58

ETCG 68

Theory Nugget

Major 6: R–3–5–6

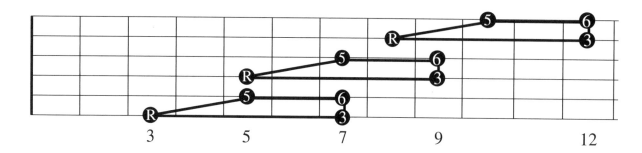

1st Inversion

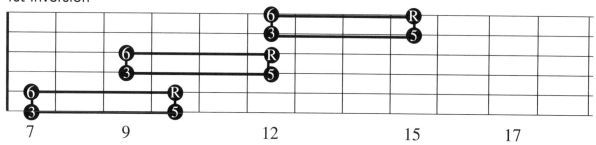

2nd Inversion

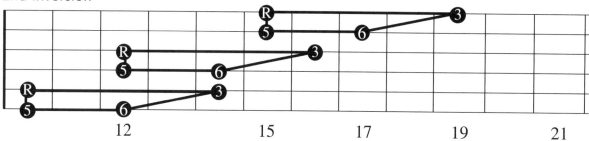

3rd Inversion

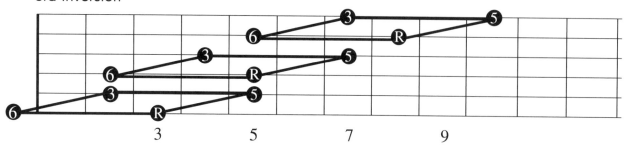

This D♭ Major exercise starts in 1st inversion.

MINOR 6

Here are two-string G Minor 6 repetitive arpeggio patterns on the three different string sets: 6–5, 4–3 and 2–1.

Theory Nugget

Minor 6: R–♭3–5–6

Root Position

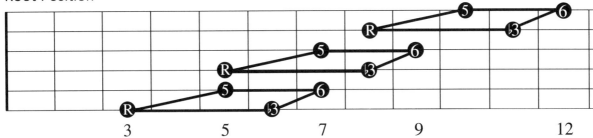

1st Inversion

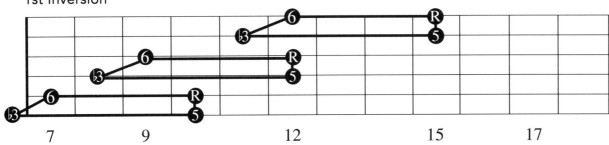

2nd Inversion

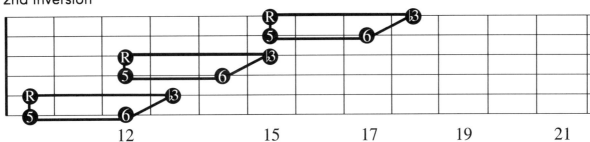

3rd Inversion

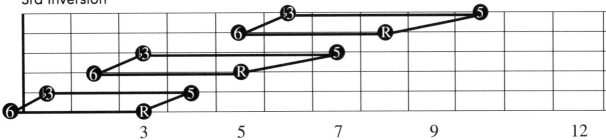

Here is a G Minor 6th arpeggio exercise.

MAJOR 7

Since there are no altered tones in the Maj7 chord, the sound is very harmonious and pleasant.

TCG 37, 41
ETCG 32, 35–36

Theory Nugget

Major 7: R–3–5–7

Root Position

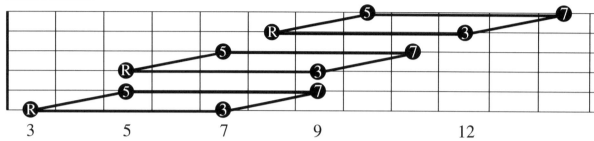

1st Inversion

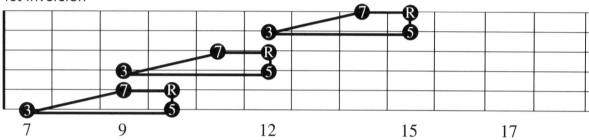

2nd Inversion

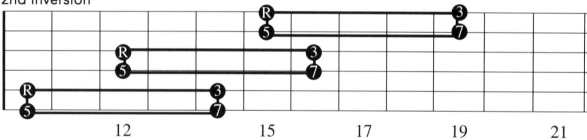

3rd Inversion

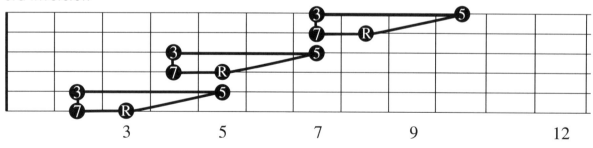

Here is a D Major 7 arpeggio exercise.

MINOR/MAJOR 7

Like the augmented arpeggio, this one is mostly used in a passing fashion often against an ascending or descending walking bass line.

TCG 50
ETCG 55

Theory Nugget

Minor/Major 7: R–♭3–5–7

Root Position

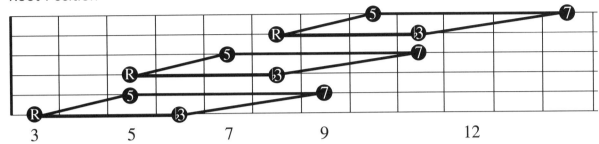

1st Inversion

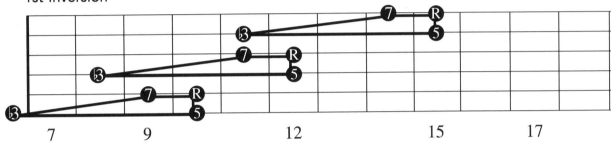

2nd Inversion

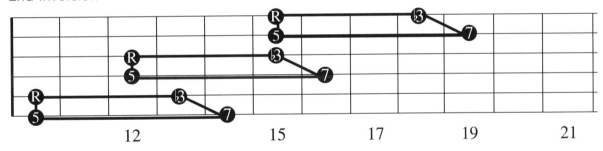

3rd Inversion

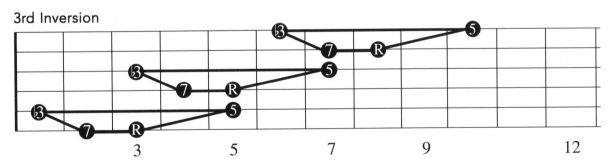

This FminMaj7 arpeggio exercise calls for hammer-ons and pull-offs. Notice the alternation between the minor (♭3) and major (♮7) sounds.

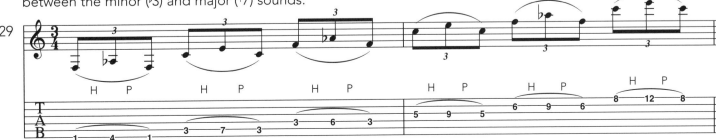

DOMINANT 7

You can use this arpeggio in conjunction with the Mixolydian mode or the blues scale for a different sounding melodic line

TCG 37, 41
ETCG 33, 38–39

Theory Nugget

Dominant 7: R–3–5–♭7

Root Position

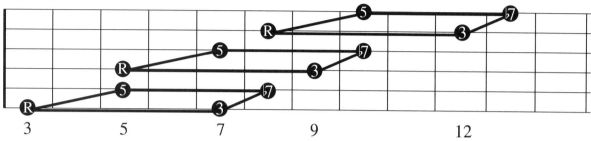

1st Inversion

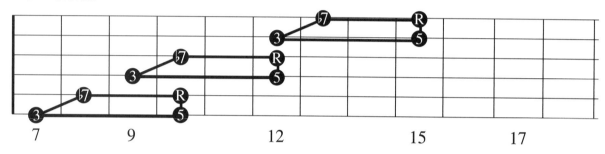

2nd Inversion

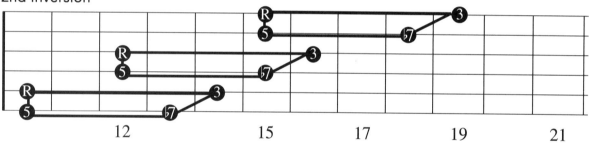

3rd Inversion

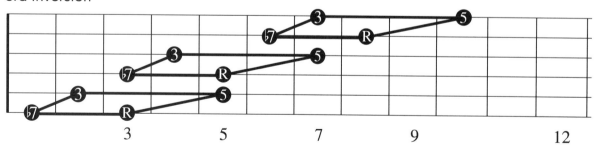

This C7 arpeggio has an angular sound because it has the notes of the dominant 7 chord out of order, skipping, for example, from 3 to 5 and then 5 to ♭7, and so on.

26

DOMINANT 7♭5

Dominant 7♭5 arpeggios are fairly dark sounding.

TCG 73

ETCG 86

Theory Nugget

Dominant 7♭5: R–3–♭5–♭7

Root Position

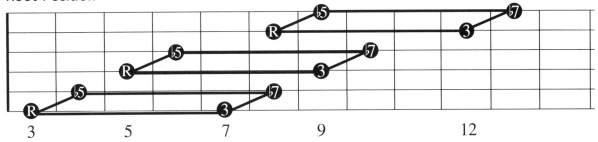

1st Inversion

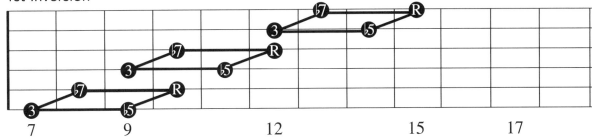

2nd Inversion

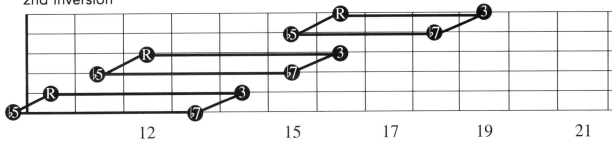

3rd Inversion

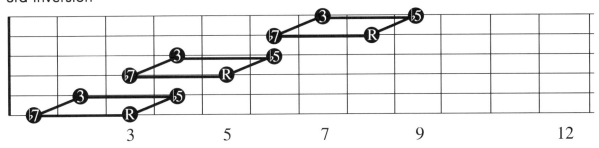

This dominant 7♭5 arpeggio exercise in A♭ also skips around in the arpeggio patterns.

Dominant 7♯5

This arpeggiation of an altered dominant can be used in conjunction with a Mixolydian scale in either a major or minor key.

TCG 73

ETCG 87

Theory Nugget

Dominant 7♯5: R–3–♯5–♭7

Root Position

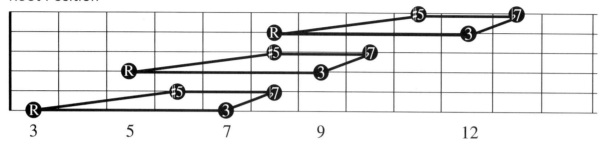

1st Inversion

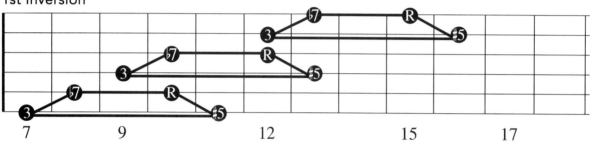

2nd Inversion

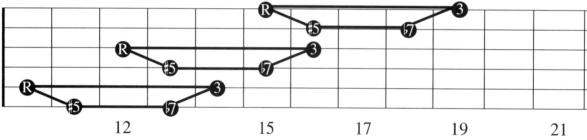

3rd Inversion

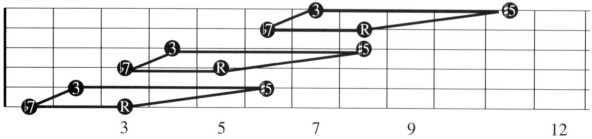

Try this G Dominant 7♯5 arpeggio exercise.

MINOR 7
The Minor 7th chord is a very common Chord and Arpeggio

TCG 37, 41
ETCG 37

Theory Nugget

Minor 7: R–♭3–5–♭7

Root Position

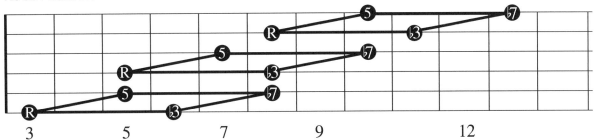

1st Inversion

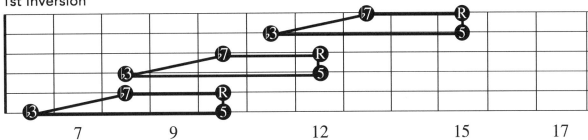

2nd Inversion

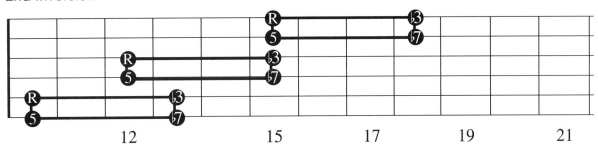

3rd Inversion

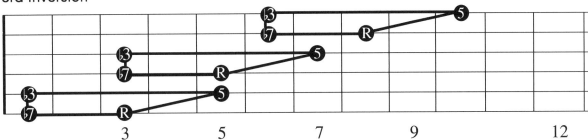

This is an E Minor 7 arpeggio exercise starting in 1st inversion.

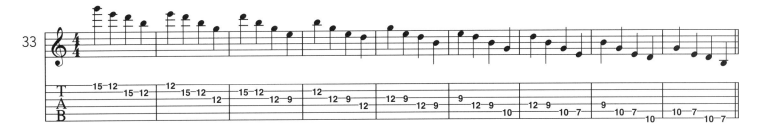

MINOR 7♭5

This dark-sounding arpeggio is diatonic in a major key.

TCG 37, 41

ETCG 40–41

Theory Nugget
Minor 7♭5: R–♭3–♭5–♭7

Root Position

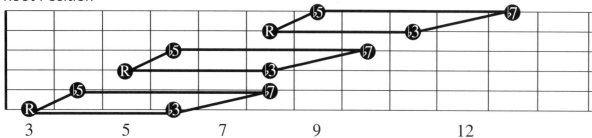

1st Inversion

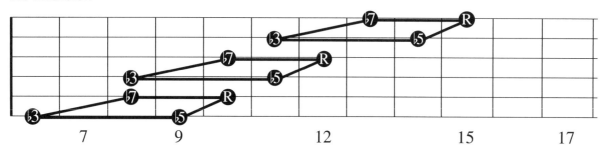

2nd Inversion

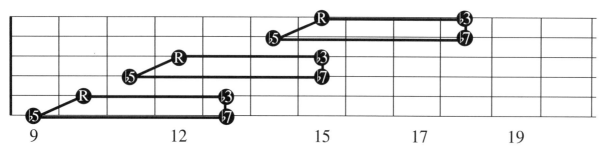

3rd Inversion

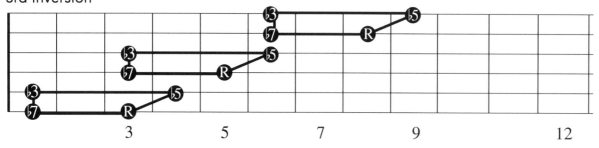

Here is an interesting exercise for the F Minor 7♭5 arpeggio.

SUSPENDED 7

This less-commonly used arpeggio has a light and airy sound.

TCG 62
ETCG 74

Theory Nugget
Suspended 7: R–4–5–♭7

Root Position

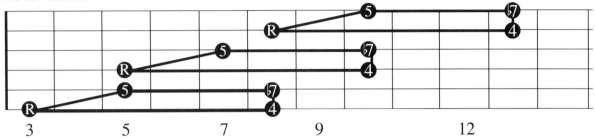

1st Inversion

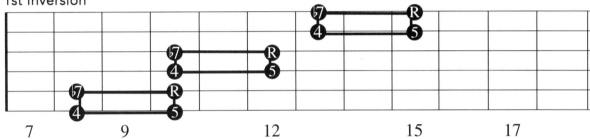

2nd Inversion

3rd Inversion

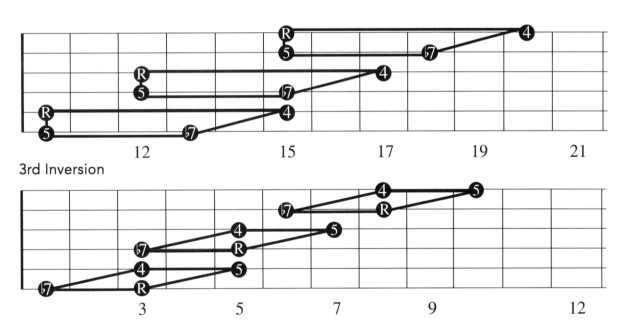

Play this A Suspended 7 exercise.

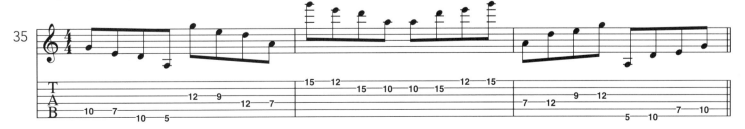

The arpeggio patterns in the next few pages do not have the same repetitive patterns as the previous. Not all of the chord tones are repeated throughout each pattern, so they are not considered complete. For example, in the major 9 arpeggio, instead of R–3–5–7–9–R–3–5–7–9 and so on, we have R–3–5–7–9–3–5–7–9. The second root is skipped in the pattern. These arpeggios still outline their corresponding chords and work well for improvising.

> TCG 59
>
> ETCG 69

MAJOR 9

Once you've played each arpeggio, you can finish by coming back down to play the root to anchor the sound (this final root is in parenthesis).

> **Theory Nugget**
> Major 9: R–3–5–7–9

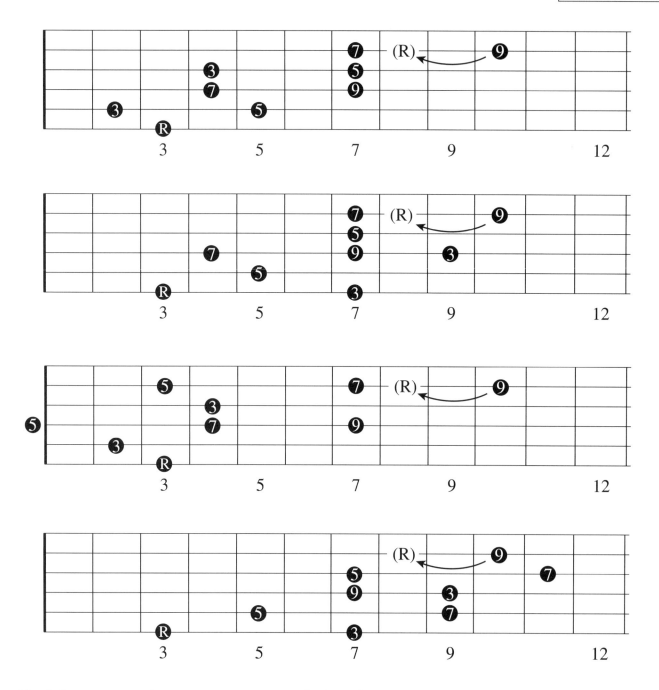

The following major 9 arpeggio exercise is in the key of G.

MINOR 9

Try this minor 9th arpeggio in combination with a Dorian, Aeolian or minor pentatonic scale.

TCG 59
ETCG 69

Theory Nugget

Minor 9: R–♭3–5–♭7–9

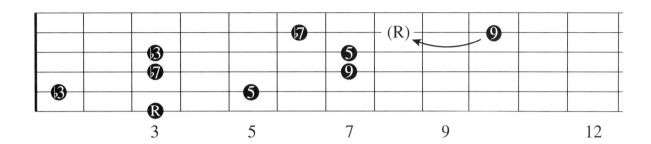

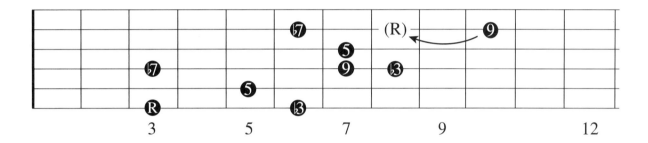

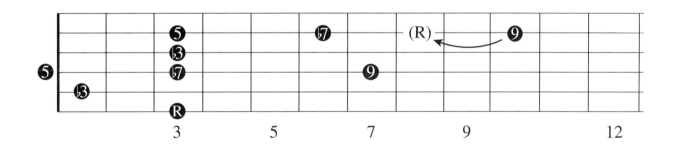

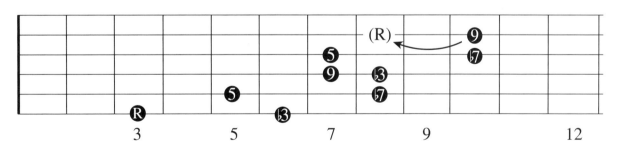

The following minor 9th arpeggio exercise starts in F then goes to G in the second bar.

DOMINANT 9

Dominant 9th arpeggios can be played along with a major or minor pentatonic scale, a blues scale or the Mixolydian mode. You can also try it with the Dorian mode.

TCG 59

ETCG 70

Theory Nugget

Dominant 9: R–3–5–♭7–9

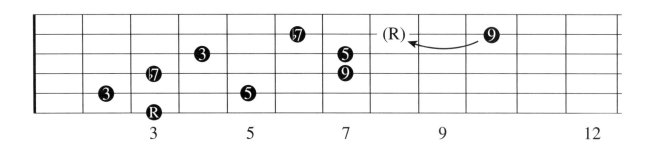

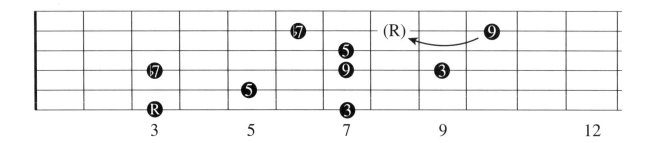

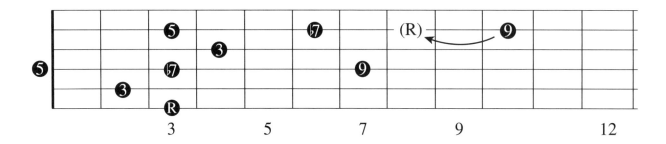

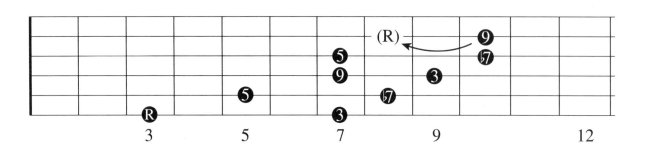

Try this A♭ Dominant 9th arpeggio exercise.

Minor 11

This is also an uncommon arpeggio but it has a very nice, jazzy character.

TCG 59

ETCG 70

Theory Nugget

Minor 11: R–♭3–5–♭7–9–11

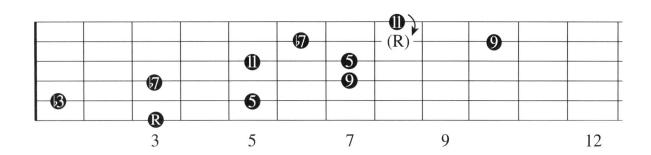

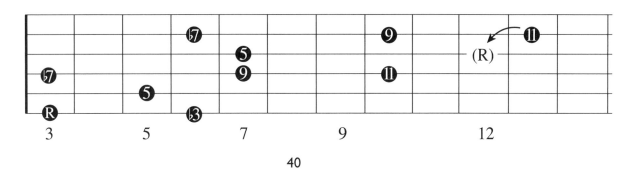

40

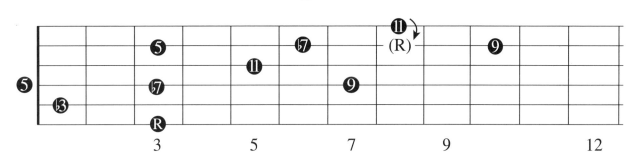

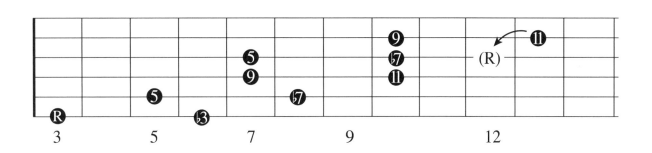

Try this F Minor 11th arpeggio exercise.

DOMINANT 11

Dominant 11th arpeggios are not as common as others and are most useful in a jazz context.

Theory Nugget

Dominant 11: R–3–5–♭7–9–11

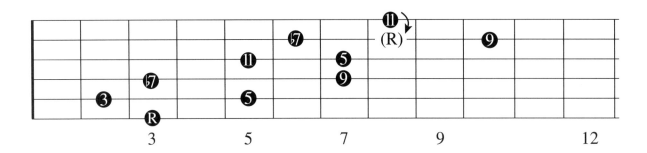

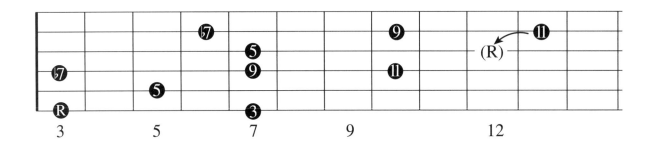

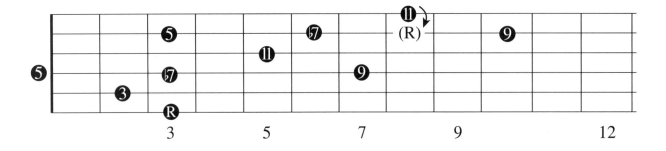

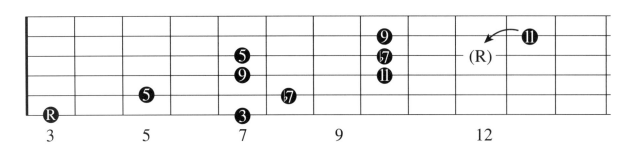

Here is a C Dominant 11th arpeggio exercise.

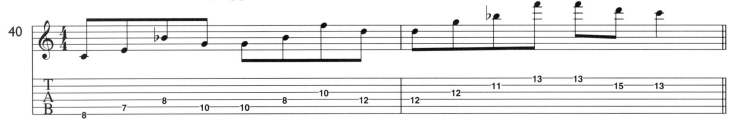

MAJOR 13

The major 13th arpeggio also has a smooth, jazzy sound.

TCG 60

ETCG 71

Theory Nugget

Major 13: R–3–5–7–9–11–13

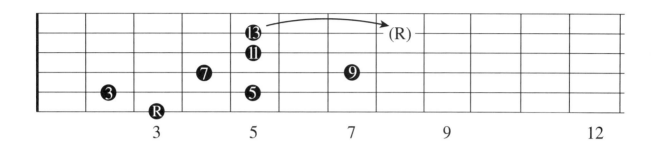

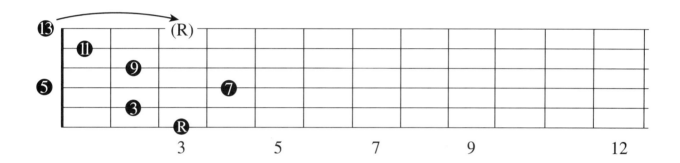

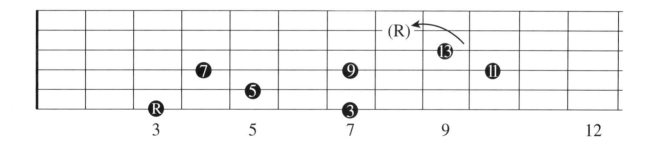

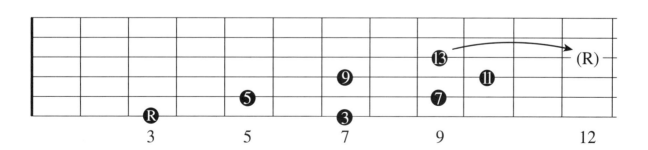

Play this jazzy G Major 13th arpeggio exercise.

MINOR 13

Use these minor 13th arpeggio patterns over the min13 harmony.

Theory Nugget

Minor 13: R–♭3–5–♭7–9–11–13

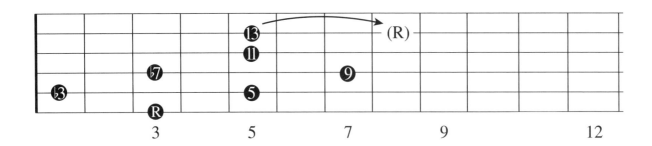

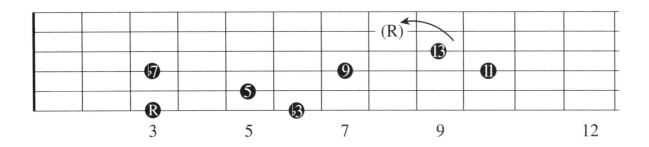

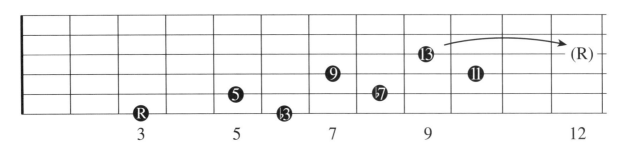

Try this A♭ Minor 13th arpeggio exercise.

DOMINANT 13

This is the last, but not least, arpeggio. The dominant 13th arpeggio works best when played over a dominant 13th chord.

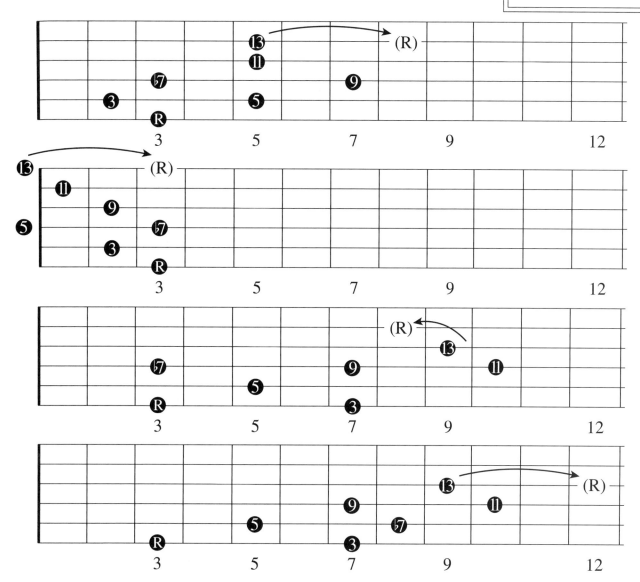

TCG 60

ETCG 72

Theory Nugget

Dominant 13: R–3–5–♭7–9–11–13

Here is a dominant 13th arpeggio in F, G and A.

CONCLUSIONS AND REVIEW:

1. An arpeggio is the notes of a chord played individually.

2. Use arpeggios during solos over chords of the same name.

3. Arpeggios create interesting melodic lines.

Congratulations! You have accomplished a great deal. Your fretboard should be starting to feel like an old, familiar friend. You are not, and will never be, completely done with this work. Use the idea of repetitive patterns with every new idea you encounter. This will allow your playing to grow endlessly. The sky is the limit!